MUS

CULTIVATION

Your All-in-One Guide to Growing, Harvesting, and Cooking Mushrooms, Indoors, Outdoors, and Beyond

Finnian Mycora

TABLE OF CONTENTS

FOREWORD..9

Why Mushrooms Matter: A Brief Overview 9

Introduction...11

What This Book Offers You 13

How to Use This Book...15

Part I: The World of Mushrooms 19

Chapter 1: The Mushroom Universe.................19

The Importance of Fungi in Our Ecosystem..................................... 20

Edible vs. Medicinal vs. Toxic: Know Your Mushrooms..........................22

Chapter 2: Why Grow Your Own Mushrooms?..............25

Health Benefits...26

Environmental Impact... 28

Financial Savings.. 30

Part II: Getting Started 33

Chapter 3: Planning Your Mushroom Adventure 33

Setting Your Cultivation Goals 34

Indoor vs. Outdoor Cultivation: Pros and Cons 36

The Budget: What to Expect..39

Chapter 4: Tools of the Trade.................................... 43

Essential Equipment and Where to Get Them 44

DIY Tools and Equipment: Save Money, Gain Skills 46

Part III: The Nitty-Gritty of Mushroom Cultivation 51

Chapter 5: The Science of Mycology 51

Understanding Mycelium and Substrates 52

The Role of Sterilization and Pasteurization 54

Chapter 6: From Spore to Harvest 59

Spore Collection and Storage.. 60

Inoculation Techniques: Beginner to Advanced.................................62

The Incubation and Fruiting Phases 65

Chapter 7: Troubleshooting and Solutions 69

Common Mistakes and How to Avoid Them 70

What to Do When Things Go Wrong 72

Part IV: Beyond Basic Cultivation 77

Chapter 8: Advanced Techniques 77

Grain-to-Grain Transfers 78

Liquid Culture Inoculation 80

Bulk Grows for Larger Yields 82

Chapter 9: Commercial Cultivation 87

Scaling Up Your Operations 88

Marketing and Selling Your Produce 90

Ethical and Sustainable Practices 93

Part V: Harvesting and Beyond 97

Chapter 10: Harvesting and Storage 97

When and How to Harvest 98

Post-Harvest Procedures and Storage 100

Chapter 11: Cooking and Enjoying Your Harvest 105

Simple and Delicious Mushroom Recipes 106

    MUSHROOM SOUP WITH THYME 106

    PORTOBELLO MUSHROOM BURGER 107

    STUFFED MUSHROOMS WITH GOAT CHEESE AND HERBS 108

    MUSHROOM AND SPINACH LASAGNA 109

    CREAMY MUSHROOM AND CHICKEN PASTA 110

    MUSHROOM AND CARAMELIZED ONION TART 111

    GRILLED MUSHROOMS WITH HERB BUTTER 112

    MUSHROOM POLENTA BITES 113

    ASIAN MUSHROOM STIR-FRY 114

    MUSHROOM AND WALNUT PÂTÉ 115

    MUSHROOM AND HERB OMELETTE 116

    BAKED MUSHROOM AND SPINACH FLATBREAD 116

Preserving Your Mushrooms: Drying, Canning, and More 117

Part VI: Additional Resources 121

Chapter 12: Mycological Communities and Further Learning 121

Joining Mushroom Clubs and Online Communities 122

Recommended Books, Journals, and Websites 124

Chapter 13: The Future of Mushroom Cultivation 129

Technological Advances 130

The Role of Mushrooms in Sustainability 132

Appendices 137

A: Glossary of Mycological Terms 138

B: Comprehensive List of Mushroom Varieties 140

C: Additional Online Resources and Supplier Directory 147

D: Frequently Asked Questions (FAQs) 150

Conclusion 155

Your Journey from Novice to Expert 155

FOREWORD

As dawn breaks over a dew-kissed forest, the ground beneath the towering trees begins to stir with life not of the animal kind, but something equally vital and often overlooked: mushrooms. This early morning scene captures the essence of what awaits us—a world where nature's quiet architects tirelessly work, shaping ecosystems and offering solutions to some of our most pressing environmental challenges.

Mushrooms, in their myriad forms, are more than just a culinary delight. They are pivotal to our understanding of sustainable living, promising avenues for both food security and ecological restoration. This book, your guide through the dense and enchanting forest of mycology, aims not just to instruct but to inspire. Here, you'll learn not only how to cultivate your own mushrooms but also why these practices matter in the larger tapestry of life.

My journey into mushroom cultivation began as a humble quest for organic, sustainable food options but quickly grew into a profound respect for these organisms' role in our world. Each chapter of this book is designed to bring you closer to understanding how mushrooms can be nurtured and harvested responsibly, how they can enhance our health, and how they contribute to a more sustainable planet.

In this guide, I invite you to join me in the delicate dance of growth and decay that mushrooms so beautifully exemplify. From the science of spores to the joy of the harvest, this book aims to equip you with the knowledge and skills to embark on your own mycological adventure, nurturing a deeper connection with nature and perhaps, a new way of looking at the world around us.

WHY MUSHROOMS MATTER: A BRIEF OVERVIEW

In the labyrinth of nature's creations, mushrooms stand out as both ancient and profoundly futuristic. Their story is woven deeply into the tapestry of life on Earth, suggesting a past as mysterious as their promise for the future. Understanding why mushrooms matter requires a journey into the heart of ecosystems, global health, and our very homes.

Mushrooms—or fungi—are among the oldest forms of life, emerging more than a billion years ago. They are not plants, though they share the ground beneath our feet. They are distinct, belonging to their own kingdom entirely, one that is critical to life as we know it. Fungi are master decomposers. Without them, Earth's landscapes would be buried in several feet of debris. They break down organic matter, recycling it back into the ecosystem, making nutrients available to other forms of life—an essential process for sustaining the planet's biomes.

The ecological roles of fungi are vast and varied. Beyond decomposition, they form symbiotic relationships with plants, including most crops, enhancing their growth and resilience to stress, such as drought or disease. These relationships, known as mycorrhizal partnerships, are fundamental to agriculture and the natural growth processes of nearly 90% of plant species. This invisible interaction happens beneath our feet, in the complex web of life where fungi lend their prowess to plant roots, aiding in water and nutrient absorption, thus ensuring the survival of forests, prairies, and agricultural fields.

The benefits of mushrooms extend far beyond their environmental roles. They are a powerhouse of nutrition and medicinal properties. Nutritionally, mushrooms are high in protein, vitamins, and minerals, while low in calories and fat, making them an excellent addition to any diet. Certain species of mushrooms have been found to contain potent medicinal properties, including boosting immune function and potentially reducing the risk of serious health conditions such as Alzheimer's, heart disease, cancer, and more. The research into these properties is burgeoning, revealing each year more about the complex bioactive compound's mushrooms contain.

Mushrooms also embody a sustainable source of food. Compared to the resources required for livestock and even some crop production, mushrooms are remarkably efficient. They can be grown on a variety of substrates, many of which are byproducts of other industries, including sawdust, agricultural waste, and even coffee grounds. This ability makes mushroom cultivation a low-waste endeavor, which is crucial in our efforts to feed a growing population without further harming the planet.

Yet, the significance of mushrooms does not end with their environmental or health benefits. They hold a cultural weight in many societies, featured prominently in culinary traditions, folk medicine, and even spiritual practices. From the truffle, a high-end culinary delight hunted in the wooded areas of Europe, to the humble button mushroom savored in dishes across the globe, mushrooms touch various aspects of human culture and cuisine.

Moreover, in recent years, the role of mushrooms in biotechnology has come to the forefront. Innovators are exploring how mycelium can be used to create sustainable alternatives to plastics, textiles, and building materials. Mycelium, the root-like structure of fungi, grows quickly and can be shaped into various forms, making it an ideal candidate for organic, biodegradable materials. These developments not only open up new avenues for reducing waste but also enhance our ability to live in harmony with nature.

As we delve deeper into the potential of mushrooms, it becomes clear that they offer us a lens through which to reimagine our relationship with nature. They challenge us to reconsider our environmental impacts, our health choices, and our technological innovations. They are not merely organisms to study but are allies in our quest for a sustainable future.

So, why do mushrooms matter? They are not just a food or an ecological component; they are a bridge to a more sustainable and health-conscious life. Each mushroom grown and harvested is a step towards understanding the delicate balance of our ecosystems. They teach us about interconnectivity, resilience, and the unsung power of the natural world.

As we turn the pages of this book, we explore not just the how's of growing mushrooms but the whys. We dive into the intricate dance of life that mushrooms partake in, and we learn how, through understanding and cultivating them, we can tap into their vast potential. This journey is about more than cultivation; it's about integrating mushrooms into the fabric of our lives, embracing their multifaceted roles, and, ultimately, crafting a future that is as sustainable as it is hopeful. Through this guide, we embark on a path that is both enlightening and essential, driven by the profound implication's mushrooms have on our world and the ways we choose to inhabit it.

INTRODUCTION

Imagine a morning walk through a damp forest, the earth soft underfoot, the air fresh with the scent of moss and ancient wood. As you walk, your eyes catch a glimpse of something extraordinary on the forest floor—a cluster of wild mushrooms, their caps like small umbrellas nestled among fallen leaves. This simple yet enchanting sight offers a gateway into an incredible world, one that is often overlooked yet is integral to our planet's health and our culinary and cultural practices. This world is the focus of our journey together in this book.

Mushrooms captivate with their mystery and variety, their uses both ancient and innovative. They are beings of transformation, turning the unseen into the essential. This book is crafted not just as a manual for growing these fascinating organisms but as an invitation to explore their broader impact on our lives and the environment.

As we delve into the pages of this guide, you'll come to understand that mushrooms are not merely a hobby or a dietary choice but a deep dive into sustainability and connection with the natural world. Each chapter is structured to walk you through the intricate details of mushroom cultivation, from the basic to the complex, from the backyard to the commercial farm, and beyond into the realms of mushroom uses in cooking and industry.

This introduction serves as your starting point, setting the stage for a deeper appreciation of what mushrooms are and why they deserve our attention. It's about more than just planting and harvesting; it's about engaging with an ecosystem, contributing to biodiversity, and rethinking our place within the natural world.

Mushrooms have been on this earth far longer than humans, thriving in nearly every habitat and playing essential roles that support the foundations of life. Their ability to decompose organic matter, partner with plants, and even combat pollution, positions them as key players in ecological restoration and sustainable practices. As we learn to cultivate mushrooms, we also learn the art of stewardship, the practice of supporting life by creating environments where diverse organisms can thrive.

Furthermore, the story of mushrooms touches on themes of resilience and adaptability—qualities that are increasingly important in our changing world. They show us how to make the most of our resources, growing in places and ways that many other crops cannot, utilizing substrates that are typically considered waste. This not only reduces our environmental footprint but also offers a model for other areas of production and life.

The techniques and tales within this book are meant to empower you, the reader, to harness the potential of mushrooms for health, for cuisine, for business, and for environmental impact. Whether you are a novice curious about starting your first mushroom kit or an experienced cultivator looking to expand your operation, this book will provide the knowledge and inspiration you need to succeed.

Through the cultivation of mushrooms, we can connect with the earth in a direct and meaningful way, turning our attention to the soil that feeds us and the organisms that enrich it. This is not just agriculture; it's an act of participation in the natural world, an exercise in nurturing and being nurtured in return.

As we embark on this journey together, remember that each mushroom you grow is a step toward a greater understanding of the environment and your role within it. It's a step toward healthier eating, more sustainable living, and a deeper connection to the world around you.

WHAT THIS BOOK OFFERS YOU

Venturing into the realm of mushroom cultivation opens a door to more than just a hobby; it unveils a path to deeper environmental connection and personal fulfillment. This book is designed as a comprehensive guide that will take you from a novice to a knowledgeable cultivator, not only enriching your diet but potentially enhancing your approach to sustainable living. Here is what this book offers you, outlined not in rigid lists but as promises of journeys we'll embark upon together.

First, you will gain a solid grounding in the basics of mycology—the study of fungi. Understanding the fundamental biology of mushrooms sets the stage for successful cultivation. You'll learn about the lifecycle of fungi, from spore to full-grown mushroom, and how this lifecycle can be nurtured in your own space, whether it be a small apartment or a sprawling backyard. This knowledge is not just academic; it's practical and geared towards helping you make informed decisions as you grow your own mushrooms.

As we delve deeper, the book offers detailed instructions on setting up your cultivation area, choosing the right substrates (the material on which mushrooms grow), and maintaining the ideal conditions for different types of fungi. These chapters are more than just how-toes; they are crafted to bring clarity to complex processes, demystifying the art and science of mushroom growing. Whether you're interested in growing common varieties like button mushrooms or venturing into more exotic types like shiitake or oyster mushrooms, this book provides step-by-step guides that are easy to follow and adapt to your needs.

But growing mushrooms is only part of the story. This book also explores the potential challenges and solutions in mushroom cultivation. You'll learn about common issues like contamination, how to prevent them, and how to address them if they arise. This section is designed to build your confidence, equipping you with the knowledge to troubleshoot problems and succeed in your cultivation endeavors.

Beyond cultivation, this book addresses harvesting and storage techniques that maximize the freshness and longevity of your mushrooms. Understanding when and how to harvest, and how to store your mushrooms, whether for immediate consumption or future use, is crucial. These techniques ensure that the fruits of your labor are enjoyed to their fullest, in flavor and nutritional value.

Additionally, this book recognizes that mushroom cultivation is not just about producing food. It's also about creating sustainable practices. You'll find discussions on how to integrate mushroom cultivation into a sustainable lifestyle, with insights into the environmental benefits of growing mushrooms, such as reducing waste and contributing to soil health. These discussions are aimed at empowering you to make choices that align with ecological stewardship and personal ethics.

For those with a culinary interest, there's a bounty to be found in the chapters dedicated to cooking and enjoying mushrooms. From simple recipes that highlight the unique flavors of freshly harvested mushrooms to more complex dishes that integrate mushrooms into diverse cuisines, this book aims to inspire your kitchen creativity. Additionally, it covers methods of preserving mushrooms, such as drying and canning, ensuring that you can enjoy your harvest year-round.

Lastly, this book doesn't end with the final chapter. It aims to be a gateway to a larger community of mushroom enthusiasts. You'll find resources for connecting with others who share your interest in fungi, from local clubs to online forums. Engaging with a community not only enhances your knowledge and enjoyment but also supports your continuous learning and involvement in the field of mycology.

This book is structured to be your companion in the journey of mushroom cultivation. It's crafted to guide, educate, and inspire you, regardless of your starting point. With each page, you'll find yourself better equipped to embark on your own path of fungal exploration, grounded in the understanding that each small step in learning to grow mushrooms is a step towards a more connected and sustainable way of living.

HOW TO USE THIS BOOK

Embarking on the journey of mushroom cultivation, with this book in your hands, is akin to having a trusted guide by your side. This text is designed not just as a collection of information, but as a dynamic tool tailored to enhance your understanding and practice of growing mushrooms. Whether you're flipping through the pages out of sheer curiosity or with a determined plan to start your own mushroom garden, here's how to make the most out of this comprehensive guide.

This book is structured to gradually build your knowledge, skill, and confidence. It starts with foundational concepts and moves towards more advanced techniques. Each chapter builds on the previous one, yet is distinct enough to stand alone. This allows you to either read the book from cover to cover or dive directly into sections that most interest you or meet your immediate needs.

Beginners might find it most helpful to start at the beginning where fundamental concepts and techniques are discussed. This will provide you with a solid base of knowledge and prepare you for the more complex topics covered in later chapters. If you're already familiar with basic mycology, you might choose to skip ahead to sections that cover new ground for you, such as advanced cultivation techniques or specific problems you're encountering.

Throughout the book, sidebars and callouts are used to highlight important tips and cautionary advice. These are meant to draw your attention to critical pieces of information that can aid in avoiding common mistakes or to underscore innovative techniques that might enhance your cultivation practice. Look for these as you navigate through the chapters, as they often provide quick, accessible insights that are immediately applicable.

Each chapter concludes with a summary that recaps the key points. These summaries are useful for review and can serve as quick references when you need to refresh your memory without rereading the entire chapter. They are especially helpful if you use the book intermittently, providing touchpoints to reacquaint yourself with the material.

Practical examples are scattered throughout the text to give you a clearer understanding of how theoretical concepts apply in real-world scenarios. These examples are drawn from actual experiences—successes and challenges alike—and are intended to give you a holistic view of what mushroom cultivation involves. They can also spark ideas on how to adapt the techniques to your own circumstances.

For those who are particularly interested in the nuances of different mushroom species, there is detailed coverage on the characteristics and specific needs of various types. This information is crucial for choosing the right species to cultivate based on your environment, goals, and resources. Each species profile is detailed enough to inform your choice, helping you to align it with your personal or commercial objectives.

The appendices at the end of the book are designed as quick-reference materials. Here you'll find a glossary of terms, a comprehensive list of mushroom varieties, and additional resources including websites and supplier directories. These resources are invaluable for deepening your knowledge and connecting with the broader mycological community.

This book also acknowledges that learning is an ongoing process. Thus, it encourages ongoing engagement with the subject through recommended readings, websites for further exploration, and tips on connecting with online and local mycological communities. Engaging with these communities can provide support, deepen your knowledge, and keep you updated on the latest in the field of mycology. To use this book most effectively, consider keeping a journal of your mushroom cultivation journey. Record your initial goals, the steps you take, observations, and outcomes. Refer back to the book as you progress, noting insights gained and new questions that arise. This reflective practice can enhance your learning experience and provide a personalized roadmap as you advance in your cultivation skills.

Finally, let this book serve not just as a guide, but as an inspiration. Let it ignite your curiosity and motivate you to explore the diverse and fascinating world of mushrooms. Whether for personal satisfaction, economic gain, or environmental contribution, the journey of mushroom cultivation is rewarding, filled with constant learning and discovery. Enjoy every step of this unique adventure, with this book as your comprehensive companion.

CHAPTER 1: THE MUSHROOM UNIVERSE

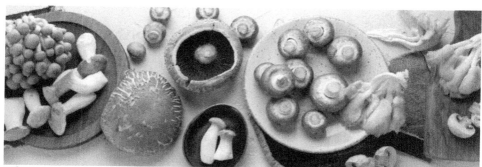

Welcome to the intriguing world of mushrooms, a realm as expansive and mysterious as the universe itself. This first chapter is designed to pull back the curtain on the rich tapestry of fungi, revealing their diverse roles and the profound impact they have on our planet. As we embark on this exploration, you will discover that mushrooms are not merely an accessory to the forest floor but are fundamental components of life on Earth.

Mushrooms have captivated humans for thousands of years, weaving their way into our myths, medicines, and meals. They are organisms of transformation, turning decay into life and presenting us with both culinary delights and ecological benefits. In this chapter, we will journey through the "Mushroom Universe," exploring the vital functions these organisms perform—from recycling nutrients to forging symbiotic relationships that nourish our world's forests.

You'll learn how mushrooms can teach us about sustainability and resilience, often thriving in places where other organisms cannot. Their ability to adapt and survive, breaking down toxic pollutants and healing damaged environments, positions them as unsung heroes of the natural world. This chapter will not only introduce you to the types of mushrooms that populate our planet but will also highlight their unseen activities that quietly sustain life as we know it.

As we delve into this chapter, imagine yourself as an explorer uncovering hidden treasures. Each section is crafted to enrich your understanding and appreciation of mushrooms, inspiring awe for their complexities and the delicate balance they help maintain in our ecosystems. This journey through the mushroom universe is just the beginning, setting the stage for deeper insights into how you can engage with and benefit from the fascinating world of fungi. Whether you are a seasoned mycologist or a curious newcomer, there is something here for everyone to marvel at and learn from. Let's step into this universe together, with eyes wide open to the wonders it holds.

THE IMPORTANCE OF FUNGI IN OUR ECOSYSTEM

Fungi, the group of organisms to which mushrooms belong, are often overlooked in the popular discourse about biodiversity and ecology, yet their importance to our ecosystems is nothing short of monumental. To fully appreciate the breadth of their roles, one must delve into the ecological functions they perform, which range from nutrient cycling to forming symbiotic relationships that sustain much of the life on our planet.

In every handful of forest soil, fungi are at work, serving as the unsung heroes of nutrient cycling. They break down complex organic materials, such as fallen leaves, dead trees, and even animal carcasses, into simpler forms that plants and other organisms can readily absorb. This decomposition process is crucial, as it prevents the accumulation of dead material, which could inhibit new growth, and recycles nutrients that are essential for the ecosystem's health. Without fungi, our forests, prairies, and even aquatic environments would be very different places, likely dominated by piles of undecomposed debris, and significantly less vibrant.

Moreover, fungi extend their influence through their symbiotic relationships with plants. Most notably, mycorrhizal fungi form partnerships with plant roots, facilitating water and nutrient uptake for their hosts, while receiving carbohydrates produced by the plant through photosynthesis. This mutualistic relationship is found in about 90% of Earth's plant species, including many crops, highlighting how integral fungi are not just to natural ecosystems but also to our agricultural systems. Mycorrhizal fungi help plants to better absorb nutrients, such as phosphorus and nitrogen, and even enhance their resistance to pathogens and environmental stresses. This relationship underscores a fundamental ecological principle: interconnectedness and interdependence.

Fungi are not only recyclers and partners but also pioneers and healers. In environments devastated by pollution, certain fungi demonstrate remarkable abilities to detoxify soils and water. Known as microembolization, this process involves fungi breaking down or absorbing pollutants, including pesticides, heavy metals, and even oil spills. By deploying fungi in contaminated sites, scientists and environmentalists harness natural processes to cleanse environments that have been damaged by industrial activity or accidents. This emerging field offers promising avenues for ecological restoration and is a testament to the innovative applications of mycological research.

The protective role of fungi extends beyond environmental cleanup. Fungi are also pivotal in preventing soil erosion. By creating dense networks of mycelium—thread-like structures that comprise the main body of a fungus—they bind soil particles together, enhancing the soil's structural integrity and its ability to retain water. This not only prevents erosion but also improves the soil's fertility, making it more conducive to plant growth. In this way, fungi contribute to the stabilization of ecosystems, proving that their impact is as foundational as it is far-reaching.

Fungi influence more than just the physical environment; they affect biodiversity as well. The diversity of fungal species within an ecosystem can be a key indicator of that ecosystem's health. Rich fungal diversity often correlates with high biodiversity overall, as fungi create niches for myriad other organisms, from bacteria and insects to mammals and birds. Each fungal species interacts with its environment in a unique way, thus contributing to the ecological complexity and resilience against disturbances like climate change or habitat loss.

Considering their crucial ecological roles and the benefits they provide, it's clear that fungi are fundamental to sustaining life on Earth as we know it. Yet, despite their importance, fungi are among the least understood and most underappreciated organisms in the biodiversity and conservation discussions. This gap in awareness and understanding is something that mycologists and ecologists are striving to address through education and research.

In bringing to light the myriad roles of fungi, this chapter not only enriches our understanding of these incredible organisms but also invites us to reflect on our own interactions with the natural world. Are we contributing to the health of our ecosystems, or are we hindering them? As we learn more about the critical functions' fungi perform, we are also called upon to consider how our actions—such as the use of pesticides, habitat destruction, and pollution—affect these vital members of our ecological communities.

By appreciating and supporting the health of fungal populations, we support the entire web of life, underscoring the profound connection between our well-being and the health of the planet. Fungi, with their intricate roles and far-reaching impacts, teach us about the delicate balance of ecosystems and our place within them. As we continue to explore the mushroom universe, let us keep in mind the fundamental ecological lessons these organisms impart, and strive to live in a way that honors and sustains the rich tapestry of life they help weave.

EDIBLE VS. MEDICINAL VS. TOXIC: KNOW YOUR MUSHROOMS

Within the vast and varied world of fungi, mushrooms distinguish themselves not only by their intriguing shapes and sizes but also by their diverse implications for human use and health. Knowing whether a mushroom is edible, medicinal, or toxic is essential for anyone venturing into their cultivation or foraging. This knowledge not only ensures safety but also enriches our understanding of how mushrooms can be integrated into our diets and wellness routines.

The allure of edible mushrooms is undeniable. From the common button mushroom to the esteemed truffle, edible fungi are celebrated for their distinctive flavors and textures. These mushrooms are not just culinary delights; they're packed with nutrients, offering a rich source of protein, vitamins, and minerals while being low in calories and fat. But the world of edible mushrooms extends far beyond what can be found in a grocery store. Many varieties that are considered delicacies, like morels and chanterelles, are commonly foraged from the wild. Cultivating an understanding of these mushrooms opens up a realm of gastronomic possibilities, allowing for a sustainable, local source of food that can inspire an array of dishes.

Medicinal mushrooms, on the other hand, offer profound health benefits that have been recognized in many cultures for centuries. Species such as rishi, cordyceps, and lion's mane are not typically known for their taste but rather for their therapeutic properties. These mushrooms contain bioactive compounds that can help strengthen the immune system, reduce inflammation, and even support neurological health. The interest in medicinal mushrooms has surged as modern science begins to back up these traditional uses with research, highlighting their potential in supporting mental health, enhancing physical endurance, and combating chronic illnesses.

However, the mushroom kingdom also has its darker side—mushrooms that are toxic, and sometimes fatally so. Distinguishing these from their harmless counterparts is crucial. Toxic mushrooms like the death cap and the destroying angel can be mistaken for edible varieties, and consuming them can lead to severe poisoning or even death. The symptoms of mushroom poisoning can range from mild digestive discomfort to severe organ failure, underscoring the importance of accurate identification.

Identifying mushrooms is an art and science that demands attention to detail. Edible, medicinal, and toxic mushrooms can sometimes look remarkably similar, but there are subtle differences that can be learned. Factors such as the shape of the cap, the color of the spores, the type of gills, and the habitat in which they grow are all crucial for identification. For the untrained eye, however, these distinctions can be daunting. Therefore, it is advised to never consume wild mushrooms without positive identification from a knowledgeable source, such as an experienced forager or through reliable mycological resources.

For those interested in cultivating mushrooms, understanding these categories is just as important. Cultivating edible or medicinal mushrooms not only provides personal satisfaction and potential health benefits but also offers a measure of safety since the conditions are controlled, reducing the risk of growing toxic varieties unintentionally. It also allows for specialization in certain types of mushrooms that can cater to specific culinary or medicinal interests.

Education is key in mushroom identification. Attending workshops, joining local mycological societies, and using identification apps or field guides can enhance your knowledge and confidence in distinguishing between edible, medicinal, and toxic mushrooms. These resources provide valuable information and connect you with communities of mushroom enthusiasts who share a passion for these fascinating organisms.

Moreover, understanding the ecological roles of these mushrooms enhances our appreciation of their presence in nature. Edible mushrooms often indicate healthy ecosystems, while medicinal mushrooms can point to specific environmental conditions that support their growth. Toxic mushrooms, despite their danger to humans, play significant roles in their ecosystems, often involved in decomposing organic matter or interacting with other plant and animal life in complex ways.

In summary, the diversity of mushrooms—edible, medicinal, and toxic—offers a fascinating glimpse into the complexity of nature and the potential benefits and dangers inherent in it. As we explore these categories, we become more connected to the natural world, more aware of its nuances, and better equipped to make informed decisions about the mushrooms we choose to consume or avoid. This knowledge not only enriches our culinary and medicinal practices but also deepens our respect and appreciation for the intricate web of life that mushrooms help sustain.

CHAPTER 2: WHY GROW YOUR OWN MUSHROOMS?

Imagine stepping into a space within your own home that serves as a mini-ecosystem, where small, unassuming spores give rise to a flush of mushrooms, ready for your kitchen table. Growing your own mushrooms is an empowering journey that connects you directly with the source of your food, blending the simplicity of nature with the art of cultivation. This chapter delves into the rewarding world of personal mushroom cultivation, exploring the myriad reasons why establishing your own mushroom garden is both a practical and fulfilling endeavor.

Why grow your own mushrooms? The answers stretch from the tangible to the intangible. On a practical level, cultivating your own mushrooms ensures a fresh, readily available supply of these nutritious and delicious organisms, free from the concerns of commercial harvesting practices. It offers the opportunity to experiment with varieties that are seldom found in supermarkets, adding a unique flair to your culinary creations. Beyond the plate, growing mushrooms at home can be a meditative practice, a form of connecting with nature that requires patience, care, and a touch of curiosity.

Moreover, mushroom cultivation at home is a step towards sustainability. It reduces the food miles associated with buying mushrooms transported from afar, and can even help in recycling household waste products like coffee grounds and cardboard into valuable compost used in cultivation.

This chapter will guide you through the basics of setting up your own mushroom-growing operation, from choosing the right type of mushrooms to suit your environment and needs, to the satisfaction of harvesting your first batch. Whether you are looking to enhance your diet, reduce your environmental impact, or simply engage in a new hobby, growing your own mushrooms offers a wealth of benefits and is an enriching addition to any lifestyle. Let's explore how this fascinating form of agriculture can fit into your life and space, bringing the magic of mycology into your everyday world.

HEALTH BENEFITS

Mushrooms, those often-overlooked denizens of the damp and dark, are packed with properties that can significantly boost our health. From enhancing our immune system to offering a high-quality source of protein, the health benefits of mushrooms are extensive and compelling. For those of us choosing to grow our own, these benefits are magnified by the guarantee of freshness and the absence of harmful agricultural chemicals often found on commercially grown produce.

Mushrooms are a low-calorie food that packs a nutritional punch. High in fiber and protein and low in fat, they are an excellent addition to any diet, especially for those seeking to manage their weight without sacrificing flavor or fullness. The protein in mushrooms is especially valuable as it contains all of the essential amino acids required by the body, making it a rare non-animal complete protein source.

Beyond their basic nutritional value, mushrooms are rich in important vitamins and minerals. They are one of the few non-animal sources of vitamin D, a critical nutrient that plays a crucial role in bone health and immune function. Most mushrooms contain vitamin D2, but when exposed to sunlight, they can also synthesize vitamin D3 and D4, providing a potent boost to your vitamin D intake. They are also a good source of B vitamins, including riboflavin, niacin, and pantothenic acid, which help provide energy by breaking down proteins, fats, and carbohydrates.

Mushrooms also contain powerful antioxidants like selenium and ergothioneine, which protect body cells from damage that might lead to chronic diseases and help strengthen the immune system. In addition to their antioxidant capacity, some mushrooms have anti-inflammatory properties, which can help improve the efficiency of the immune system and are linked to a reduced risk of serious health conditions such as Alzheimer's disease, heart disease, and cancer.

The medicinal properties of certain mushroom species are particularly notable. For example, rishi mushrooms are known for their immune-boosting effects and have been used in traditional Asian medicine for centuries to treat infections and more. Shiitake mushrooms, on the other hand, contain compounds that help lower cholesterol and may improve heart health. Lion's mane mushrooms have been studied for their potential neuroprotective benefits, which could be significant in treating conditions like Alzheimer's and Parkinson's disease.

Moreover, growing mushrooms at home can have a direct impact on mental health. The act of cultivating one's own food can be a deeply satisfying and therapeutic endeavor. It encourages mindfulness and stress reduction and can be a peaceful, meditative practice that contributes to overall mental wellness. Additionally, the satisfaction of watching mushrooms grow and then harvesting them can provide a sense of accomplishment and self-sufficiency.

For those of us who cultivate our mushrooms, the control over the growing environment ensures that we can maximize these health benefits. Homegrown mushrooms can be harvested at peak freshness, which not only optimizes their flavor but also their nutritional value. Furthermore, by growing mushrooms at home, cultivators can avoid the pesticides and herbicides commonly used in commercial agriculture, which can remain on mushrooms sold in stores and potentially offset some of their health benefits.

In cultivating mushrooms, you also have the opportunity to explore varieties that are not commonly available in supermarkets. Many of these less common mushrooms, such as maitake or turkey tail, have unique health benefits not found in more widely consumed varieties. For instance, maitake has been shown to help regulate blood sugar levels and enhance immune system activity, while turkey tail is well-regarded for its cancer-fighting properties due to the polysaccharopeptide it contains.

In conclusion, the health benefits of mushrooms are diverse and significant. From providing essential nutrients and bioactive compounds that promote physical health to offering psychological benefits through their cultivation, mushrooms are a valuable addition to any diet. Growing your own mushrooms enhances these benefits, allowing for greater control over your diet and introducing you to the joys of mycology. As we continue to explore the reasons for growing mushrooms, these health benefits highlight just how much these remarkable fungi have to offer.

ENVIRONMENTAL IMPACT

As we delve deeper into the motivations behind growing your own mushrooms, the environmental benefits stand out starkly, offering compelling reasons that extend beyond personal health and well-being. The cultivation of mushrooms at home can have a profound impact on reducing our ecological footprint, contributing positively to the planet's health in several significant ways.

Mushroom cultivation is remarkably resource-efficient compared to traditional crop farming. Mushrooms require minimal space and water, making them an ideal crop for urban gardeners and those with limited resources. They grow vertically and can thrive in controlled environments such as basements or containers, utilizing spaces that are unsuitable for other types of agriculture. This spatial efficiency reduces the need for clearing land, thus preserving habitats and maintaining biodiversity.

Moreover, mushrooms have a unique ability to grow on a variety of substrates that are often considered waste products. Coffee grounds, sawdust, agricultural byproducts, and even paper waste can be transformed into nutritious mushroom substrate. By utilizing these materials, mushroom growers can help reduce waste streams and promote a circular economy. This not only alleviates the pressure on landfills but also turns waste into valuable food, closing the loop in a truly sustainable fashion.

Water usage is another area were mushroom cultivation shines in terms of sustainability. Mushrooms require significantly less water than conventional crops.

Since they are typically grown in controlled environments, the water they do need can be easily managed and recycled within the system, leading to a drastic reduction in water waste. This is particularly crucial in regions where water scarcity is a pressing issue.

In addition to being low in water and space requirements, growing mushrooms can also contribute to soil health. After mushrooms have been harvested, the spent substrate, enriched with organic matter from mycelial growth, makes excellent compost. This can be returned to the garden to improve soil structure and fertility, promoting healthier plant growth and further reducing the garden's overall environmental impact.

The environmental benefits of mushroom cultivation also include a reduction in greenhouse gas emissions. Traditional agriculture, especially livestock farming, is a significant producer of methane—a potent greenhouse gas. Mushrooms emit far fewer greenhouse gases during their growth cycle. By substituting even, a small portion of our protein intake with mushrooms, we can lessen our reliance on meat and significantly decrease our carbon footprint.

Furthermore, homegrown mushrooms contribute to biodiversity. Each batch of mushrooms can serve as a living laboratory, allowing cultivators to experiment with different strains and varieties that might not be commercially available. This diversity not only enhances the resilience of home gardens but also supports a wider genetic variety of fungi, which is crucial for maintaining the ecological balance and adapting to changing environmental conditions.

The process of growing mushrooms also offers educational opportunities, raising awareness about sustainable practices and the importance of environmental stewardship. It provides a hands-on way for people of all ages to engage with principles of ecology and sustainability. Through the simple act of growing mushrooms, individuals learn about the broader implications of their food choices and the impact these choices have on the planet.

By choosing to cultivate mushrooms at home, we make a statement about the kind of world we want to live in—one that values efficiency, sustainability, and respect for nature. It's a step towards living more harmoniously with our environment, taking responsibility for our part in the global ecosystem, and actively contributing to its health.

In this way, the environmental impact of growing your own mushrooms reaches beyond the immediate benefits of reduced waste and resource use. It's about fostering a deeper connection with nature and a greater appreciation for the processes that sustain life on Earth. It's about empowering ourselves and future generations with the knowledge and skills to make positive changes, one mushroom at a time. Through these efforts, we not only enhance our own lives but also contribute to a more sustainable and environmentally conscious world.

FINANCIAL SAVINGS

In the journey of mushroom cultivation, alongside the environmental and health benefits, there lies a compelling economic advantage. Growing your own mushrooms can lead to significant financial savings, especially when considering the cost of gourmet varieties at the supermarket and the expenses associated with industrial agriculture. This subchapter explores how cultivating mushrooms at home can be a boon to your budget, turning a small investment into substantial savings over time.

The initial cost of setting up a mushroom growing operation at home is relatively low compared to many other agricultural endeavors. Basic supplies such as spores or spawn, substrate, and containers are inexpensive and readily available. Moreover, the ability to use upcycled materials for growing containers and substrates—like buckets, jars, coffee grounds, straw, or wood chips—can reduce costs even further. Once established, a mushroom cultivation setup requires minimal upkeep, which keeps ongoing expenses low.

Mushrooms have a rapid growth cycle, with some species ready to harvest within just a few weeks of starting cultivation. This quick turnaround means that for the cost of a few supplies, you can begin harvesting your own mushrooms in less time than it takes to grow most vegetables. As mushrooms can be cultivated year-round in controlled indoor environments, this allows for continuous production without the seasonal limitations associated with traditional gardening. Consequently, you can offset the cost of buying mushrooms regularly, which is particularly significant if you favor specialty varieties like shiitake, oyster, or lion's mane, which tend to carry a higher price tag in stores.

Moreover, the scalability of mushroom farming offers further economic benefits. Once you've mastered the basic techniques, expanding your operation can be done at a relatively low cost. This scalability lets you increase your yield without a proportional increase in expense. For those interested, this can even evolve from a hobby into a small business, selling excess produce at farmers' markets or directly to restaurants, creating a potential source of income.

Another financial benefit of growing your own mushrooms lies in the reduction of food waste. Mushrooms can be harvested at precisely the right time when you need them, ensuring freshness and reducing the spoilage that often occurs with store-bought mushrooms, which may have traveled long distances and been stored for extended periods. Additionally, the substrate used for growing mushrooms, once spent, can serve as an excellent addition to your compost heap, enhancing your garden's soil quality without the need to purchase commercial soil amendments.

Home cultivation also provides an educational opportunity, which can be considered a saving in learning and recreational costs. The process of growing mushrooms involves skills that once learned, can be applied in various ways— perhaps even leading to reduced costs in other areas of home gardening or self-sufficiency efforts. It's an investment in knowledge that pays dividends beyond the mushrooms themselves.

The financial implications of cultivating mushrooms at home extend to broader economic considerations as well. By reducing reliance on commercially grown mushrooms, you contribute to a decrease in the demand for industrially produced food, which often involves significant environmental costs, such as carbon emissions from transportation and chemical inputs used in large-scale agriculture. This shift not only saves money but also supports a more sustainable food system by promoting local and low-impact food production.

Growing mushrooms at home is not merely an exercise in food production; it's a financially savvy practice that aligns with a lifestyle of environmental consciousness and self-sufficiency. The savings realized from this endeavor allow for a redirection of funds perhaps towards other quality-of-life improvements or environmental initiatives, reinforcing the principle that sustainable living can be economically viable as well as ecologically responsible.

In conclusion, the financial benefits of home mushroom cultivation are manifold, offering significant savings on grocery bills, the potential for income, educational enrichment, and a reduced environmental impact. This aspect of mushroom cultivation not only enriches your diet but also supports a sustainable economic model that can enhance your financial well-being.

CHAPTER 3: PLANNING YOUR MUSHROOM ADVENTURE

Embarking on your mushroom cultivation journey is akin to setting out on a grand adventure, one that requires curiosity, preparation, and a dash of daring. This chapter is designed to serve as your roadmap, guiding you through the initial steps of planning your very own mushroom cultivation project. Whether your goal is to sprinkle freshly harvested shiitakes into your pasta, bolster your health with medicinal fungi, or simply explore the fascinating life cycle of these extraordinary organisms, proper planning is key to a rewarding experience.

Before a single spore is sown, thoughtful preparation can set the stage for success. Like any seasoned explorer, a mushroom cultivator must consider what tools are necessary, the conditions under which their chosen mushrooms will thrive, and what their ultimate goals are. This planning phase is crucial because mushrooms, though versatile, have specific needs that vary widely between species.

This chapter will walk you through assessing your available space, whether it's a small corner of a city apartment or a spacious backyard garden. You'll learn how to select the right types of mushrooms for your environment and goals. Indoor and outdoor cultivation each offer unique advantages and challenges, which you'll need to weigh based on your lifestyle and the climate you live in.

Moreover, setting your cultivation goals involves more than deciding on the species to grow. It encompasses understanding the scale of your endeavor, determining how much time and resources you are willing to invest, and what you aim to achieve—be it personal consumption, educational purposes, or perhaps a commercial venture.

As you turn these pages, think of this planning stage not just as a set of instructions, but as the beginning of a personal narrative in the world of mycology, where each decision shapes the plot of your unique cultivation story. Ready your tools and your curiosity—your mushroom adventure is about to begin.

SETTING YOUR CULTIVATION GOALS

Embarking on the journey of mushroom cultivation requires clarity about what you hope to achieve. Setting your cultivation goals is a critical first step that determines the scale, methods, and types of mushrooms you will focus on. This decision-making process is as personal as it is strategic, reflecting both your interests and the practicalities of your living environment.

Firstly, consider why you are drawn to mushroom cultivation. Are you motivated by a desire to enhance your diet with fresh, organic produce? Perhaps the medicinal properties of certain fungi have piqued your interest, or maybe you are attracted to the environmental benefits of growing your own food. For others, mushroom cultivation could be a gateway to starting a small business. Each of these motivations will guide different decisions in the cultivation process—from the choice of species to the methods of cultivation and the scale of your operation.

For home cultivators, the process often begins modestly. Many start with easy-to-grow species like oyster or button mushrooms, which do not require complex setups. This can be ideal for those looking to add fresh mushrooms to their meals regularly without significant initial investment. In these cases, your goal might be simple: establish a reliable, small-scale system that provides a steady supply of mushrooms for personal use.

On the other hand, if your interest lies in the medicinal qualities of mushrooms, such as rishi or lion's mane, your approach might involve more specialized substrates and conditions to optimize the yield and potency of your fungi. Here, the goal shifts towards maximizing the medicinal benefits, which might involve more rigorous attention to the growing environment and possibly a greater investment in specialized equipment.

For enthusiasts thinking about commercial cultivation, setting your goals involves a detailed business plan that includes market research, scaling up production, and compliance with local agricultural regulations. This level of planning ensures that once your operation is ready to expand, you have a clear understanding of the market demands and how to meet them efficiently.

Next, consider the space you have available. Do you have a small balcony, a basement, or a backyard at your disposal? The amount of available space not only influences the quantity of mushrooms you can realistically grow but also the methods you can employ. Indoor cultivation typically requires purchasing or building growth chambers and controlling environmental factors such as temperature, humidity, and light. Outdoor cultivation, while offering more space, may expose your mushrooms to more variables, such as pests and fluctuating weather conditions.

Resource availability is another crucial aspect. Assess what materials you can easily access, what you will need to purchase, and how much time you can dedicate to maintaining your mushroom garden. These factors heavily influence the complexity of your setup. For example, utilizing waste products like coffee grounds or straw as a substrate can be cost-effective and environmentally friendly, but it also requires regular replenishing and maintenance.

Time investment is a significant consideration. Mushroom cultivation can range from low-maintenance projects, like growing mushrooms in coffee grounds, to high-maintenance operations, such as managing a sterile laboratory for producing spores. Your daily and weekly routines will need to accommodate the time needed to care for your mushrooms, especially during critical phases like the incubation and fruiting periods.

Setting clear, achievable goals also involves educating yourself about potential challenges and how to address them. Understanding common issues like contamination, improper moisture levels, or inadequate nutrient supply can help you set more realistic expectations and prepare effective solutions. This proactive approach reduces frustration and increases the likelihood of a successful harvest.

As you delineate your goals, document them. Keeping a cultivation journal can be incredibly beneficial. Record your objectives, the steps you plan to take to achieve them, and any observations and outcomes along the way. This record not only helps in refining your cultivation techniques over time but also serves as a motivational tool, showing you how far you've come from your initial aspirations to the realities of your mushroom cultivation journey.

In conclusion, setting your cultivation goals is a dynamic process that balances your aspirations with the practicalities of your environment and resources. By clearly defining what you want to achieve through mushroom cultivation, you tailor the experience to fit your life and interests, paving the way for a fulfilling and productive venture into the world of fungi.

INDOOR VS. OUTDOOR CULTIVATION: PROS AND CONS

Choosing between indoor and outdoor mushroom cultivation is a pivotal decision for any aspiring mycologist. Each approach comes with its unique set of advantages and challenges, tailored to different lifestyles, climates, and goals. Understanding these pros and cons will help you make an informed decision that best suits your mushroom adventure.

Indoor Cultivation

Pros:

1. **Controlled Environment:** One of the biggest advantages of growing mushrooms indoors is the ability to control environmental conditions such as temperature, humidity, and light. This control can lead to higher yields and more predictable growth cycles, as it reduces the risks associated with pests and adverse weather.

2. **Year-Round Production:** Indoor cultivation allows for the continuous production of mushrooms, regardless of the season. This is particularly

beneficial in regions with extreme winters or summers, where outdoor conditions are not conducive to mushroom growth for part of the year.

3. **Space Efficiency:** Growing mushrooms indoors is ideal for urban dwellers or those with limited outdoor space. Mushrooms can be cultivated in containers, bags, or small boxes, utilizing spaces like basements, garages, or even closets.

Cons:

1. **Initial Setup Cost:** Setting up an indoor cultivation system can require a significant upfront investment. Costs include purchasing or building growth chambers, installing humidity and temperature control systems, and, in some cases, artificial lighting.

2. **Energy Usage:** Maintaining the right environmental conditions can consume a lot of energy, particularly if you need to artificially heat, cool, or light your growing area. This not only adds to the cost but also to the environmental footprint of your cultivation.

3. **Maintenance and Monitoring:** Indoor systems require regular monitoring and maintenance to ensure that conditions remain optimal. This can be time-consuming and requires a consistent commitment.

Outdoor Cultivation
Pros:

1. **Natural Conditions:** Outdoor mushroom cultivation makes use of natural conditions, which can help foster more robust and naturally adapted fungi. Many mushrooms prefer the subtle fluctuations in natural light and temperature, which can encourage healthier growth.

2. **Lower Start-Up Costs:** Generally, starting an outdoor mushroom farm requires less technical equipment than an indoor operation. This can make it a more accessible option for beginners or those with limited budgets.

3. **Environmental Integration:** Growing mushrooms outdoors can enhance the biodiversity of your garden. Mushrooms can help improve soil quality and decrease the need for chemical fertilizers, benefiting other plants in your garden.

Cons:

1. **Weather Dependence:** The biggest challenge of outdoor cultivation is its dependence on suitable weather conditions. Excessive rain, drought, or unexpected temperature swings can drastically affect your yield.

2. **Pest and Disease Exposure:** Outdoor mushrooms are more susceptible to pests and diseases. Slugs, insects, and competing fungi can pose significant threats to your crop.

3. **Seasonal Production:** Unlike indoor cultivation, outdoor mushroom growing is often limited to specific times of the year, typically spring and fall, when conditions are most favorable.

Choosing Your Path

When deciding whether to cultivate mushrooms indoors or outdoors, consider your local climate, your availability to manage the cultivation environment, and your personal preferences. For those in urban settings or with harsh local climates, indoor cultivation might be the best choice. However, if you have access to a protected outdoor space and prefer a more natural approach, outdoor cultivation could be more rewarding.

For beginners, experimenting with both methods on a small scale can be insightful. Start with easy-to-grow species that are less sensitive to environmental fluctuations, such as oyster mushrooms. They can thrive both indoors and outdoors, giving you a practical understanding of what each type of cultivation entails.

Incorporating both methods can also be a strategic approach. For example, spawn can be initiated indoors where conditions are controlled, and then transferred outdoors once colonized. This hybrid method combines the control of indoor cultivation with the natural benefits of the outdoors, often yielding excellent results. Ultimately, the choice between indoor and outdoor mushroom cultivation depends on aligning your cultivation goals with your personal circumstances and environmental conditions. Each method has its merits and challenges, and the best choice is one that complements your lifestyle, meets your cultivation goals, and brings joy to your mycological journey.

THE BUDGET: WHAT TO EXPECT

Embarking on your mushroom cultivation journey not only requires physical space and commitment but also a careful consideration of your budget. Whether you decide to grow mushrooms as a hobby or with commercial intentions, understanding the financial aspects is crucial. This sub-chapter aims to provide a comprehensive view of what to expect budget-wise when planning your mushroom adventure.

Initial Investment

The initial cost of setting up your mushroom cultivation project can vary widely based on several factors including the scale of your operation, the method of cultivation (indoor vs. outdoor), and the types of mushrooms you intend to grow. Here's a breakdown of the typical expenses:

1. **Spores or Spawn:** These are essential for starting your mushroom cultivation and can vary in cost. Spores generally are cheaper and used for more advanced techniques, while spawn is slightly more expensive but easier to handle and has a higher success rate for beginners.

2. **Substrate:** The medium on which your mushrooms will grow can be something as simple as straw or wood chips, or as complex as a specially formulated mushroom growing soil. Costs will vary depending on the availability of these materials in your area and the quantity required.

3. **Containers or Beds:** Whether you're growing mushrooms in bags, buckets, trays, or outdoor beds, there will be some cost associated with acquiring these containers. Repurposed materials can help keep this cost down.

4. **Environmental Control Equipment:** For indoor cultivation, equipment such as humidifiers, heaters, and ventilation fans may be necessary to create optimal growing conditions. These can be one of the larger upfront costs, especially for those aiming for a controlled indoor environment.

5. **Miscellaneous Supplies:** Other supplies might include thermometers, hygrometers, timers, and perhaps a few tools for harvesting and processing your mushrooms.

Ongoing Expenses

After the initial setup, there are several ongoing costs to consider:

1. **Utility Costs:** Especially pertinent for indoor growers, the cost of electricity to power lights, heating, and humidity control can add up. Outdoor growers might have fewer utility expenses, but still might need to consider water costs.

2. **Substrate Renewal:** Depending on the mushroom species and cultivation method, you may need to regularly replace or supplement the substrate.

3. **Spawn Replenishment:** While some growers learn to create their own spawn to save money, beginners will likely need to purchase new spawn for each growing cycle until they become more experienced.

Potential Savings and Earnings

One of the attractive aspects of mushroom cultivation is the potential for cost savings and even earnings:

1. **Reduced Grocery Bills:** Regularly harvesting your own mushrooms can significantly cut down on your grocery expenses, especially if you enjoy gourmet varieties like shiitake or oyster mushrooms, which can be costly when bought fresh.

2. **Selling Excess Produce:** If your operation produces more mushrooms than you can use, selling the excess can provide additional income. Local farmers' markets, restaurants, and health food stores may be potential markets for fresh, locally-grown mushrooms.

3. **DIY Substrate and Spawn:** As you gain experience, you might choose to prepare your own substrates and spawn from available resources, which can greatly reduce ongoing costs. For example, using spent coffee grounds as a substrate or learning to culture your own spawn from purchased mushrooms.

Budgeting Tips

1. **Start Small:** It's wise to start with a small, manageable system to minimize your initial investment and learn the ropes before scaling up.

2. **Use Repurposed Materials:** Containers and other equipment can often be sourced second-hand or repurposed from items you already have, reducing the need to buy new materials.

3. **Research and Plan:** Thorough planning and research can help avoid unnecessary expenses. Understanding what each type of mushroom requires can prevent spending on unsuitable materials or equipment.

4. **Keep Detailed Records:** Maintaining detailed records of expenses and yields not only helps in managing your budget but also in planning future expansions or adjustments to your cultivation process.

Embarking on mushroom cultivation with a clear understanding of the financial investment required can help ensure that your mushroom-growing experience is both enjoyable and economically feasible. Whether for personal satisfaction or commercial gain, being informed and prepared financially is as important as any other aspect of your mushroom cultivation plan.

CHAPTER 4: TOOLS OF THE TRADE

As you embark on the rewarding journey of mushroom cultivation, having the right tools in your arsenal is as vital as possessing the proper knowledge. Just as a carpenter needs a hammer and saw, a mushroom cultivator requires specific tools to efficiently nurture and harvest their fungal bounty. This chapter is dedicated to unraveling the 'Tools of the Trade,' ensuring you are well-equipped for the intricate yet profoundly satisfying process of growing mushrooms.

Whether you're setting up a small indoor grow space or planning to cultivate mushrooms on a larger scale outdoors, the right tools can make the difference between struggle and success. Understanding what equipment is necessary, what each tool does, and how to use them effectively will streamline your cultivation process, making it more enjoyable and fruitful.

We will explore everything from the basics, like containers and substrates, to more specialized equipment, such as humidity and temperature control devices essential for indoor cultivation. You'll learn not only what tools are needed but also how to choose the best options based on durability, efficiency, and cost-effectiveness.

This chapter will also touch on innovative ways to repurpose everyday items as mushroom cultivation tools, aligning with sustainable practices and cost-saving strategies. Sometimes, the most effective tools are those improvised from what we already have at hand, turning the ordinary into the extraordinary through creativity and ingenuity.

By the end of this chapter, you'll have a comprehensive toolkit, both literal and metaphorical, that will prepare you to cultivate mushrooms with confidence and skill. Whether you are a novice eager to grow your first batch of oyster mushrooms or a seasoned cultivator looking to refine your setup, understanding the tools of the trade is a step towards mastering the art and science of mushroom cultivation. Let's delve into the essentials and prepare you for the fascinating work ahead.

ESSENTIAL EQUIPMENT AND WHERE TO GET THEM

Embarking on the journey of mushroom cultivation means preparing to equip yourself with the essential tools that make the process not just possible, but also more efficient and enjoyable. Understanding what equipment, you need and where to find it can set your mushroom growing endeavor on a path of success from the very beginning.

1. Containers and Growing Trays: Whether you're cultivating mushrooms indoors or outdoors, containers are essential. Indoors, you might use bags, jars, or boxes, depending on the type of mushroom and the space available. Outdoors, wooden trays, raised beds, or even logs can be used for species like shiitake that grow on wood. These can be sourced from gardening stores, online marketplaces, or by repurposing items you might already have at home.

2. Substrate: The substrate is your mushroom's growing medium. Common substrates include straw, wood chips, coffee grounds, and sawdust, each suitable for different types of mushrooms. Often, local agricultural suppliers, garden centers, or even coffee shops (for used coffee grounds) are excellent places to source these materials. Ensure that any wood-based substrate is untreated to avoid chemicals that could harm your fungi.

3. Spores or Spawn: The starting material for mushroom cultivation can be spores (for more experienced growers) or spawn (for beginners and those looking for more reliability). These can be purchased from specialized online retailers that offer a wide variety of mushroom types. Choosing reputable suppliers ensures high-quality spawn that increases your chances of a successful crop.

4. Humidity and Temperature Control Systems: For indoor cultivation, maintaining the correct environment is crucial. Humidifiers, dehumidifiers, and heaters or coolers might be necessary depending on your local climate and indoor conditions. These can be found at hardware stores or online. It's vital to monitor these conditions, so a good quality hygrometer and thermometer are also essential tools.

5. Watering Equipment: Mushrooms require a moist environment to thrive. A fine mist sprayer is ideal for gently watering your mushrooms without disturbing the substrate or damaging the delicate fungi. These are available at any gardening store and are a must-have for keeping conditions optimal.

6. Lighting: If you're growing mushrooms indoors and natural light is limited, you may need artificial lighting. Mushrooms don't require much light, but certain types benefit from specific light conditions. Simple LED or fluorescent grow lights will suffice and are readily available in-home improvement stores or online.

7. Ventilation: Good airflow is essential, especially for indoor growing, to prevent the buildup of humidity and any related mold issues. Small fans or an air exchange system might be necessary, which you can find at any general hardware store.

8. Harvesting Tools: Depending on the type of mushrooms you are growing; you may need a sharp knife or scalpel for harvesting. These should be clean and sharp to make a clean cut that does not damage the mycelium and allows for future flushes of mushrooms.

9. Cleaning and Sterilization Supplies: Keeping your equipment clean is crucial in mushroom cultivation to avoid contamination. Basic cleaning supplies, along with sterilization equipment such as a pressure cooker for sterilizing substrates and tools, can be crucial. These are available at kitchen supply stores or online.

Where to Shop:

- **Local Gardening Stores:** These often carry most of the basic supplies needed for outdoor and some indoor mushroom growing setups.

- **Online Specialty Shops:** For more specific items like high-quality spawn, specialized substrates, and certain indoor cultivation equipment, look to online stores that specialize in mushroom cultivation supplies.

- **Home Improvement Stores:** A great resource for containers, tools, and environmental control systems.

- **Farm Supply Stores:** These can be excellent places for bulk substrate materials, especially if you are setting up a larger operation.

When sourcing these materials, consider the sustainability of each product, opting for eco-friendly and locally sourced materials whenever possible. Not only does this support local businesses, but it also reduces the environmental impact of your cultivation practice.

As you gather your tools and materials, keep a record of what works best for your specific situation and any modifications you make to your setup. This not only helps in refining your cultivation process but also assists in troubleshooting any issues that arise, creating a rewarding and productive mushroom growing experience.

DIY TOOLS AND EQUIPMENT: SAVE MONEY, GAIN SKILLS

Mushroom cultivation, like any hobby or agricultural pursuit, can be enhanced by a DIY approach to tools and equipment. Not only does crafting your own equipment help save money, but it also enriches your skills and deepens your understanding of the entire cultivation process. In this sub-chapter, we'll explore how you can build or repurpose items to suit your mushroom growing needs, infusing your project with a personal touch and a sense of accomplishment.

Building Your Own Growth Chambers

One of the more significant expenses in indoor mushroom cultivation is the growth chamber. However, with a bit of ingenuity, you can construct your own using items that might otherwise be discarded. An old cabinet, bookshelf, or even a large storage tote can be transformed into an effective growth chamber. The key elements to include are proper ventilation and the ability to control humidity and temperature. You can add small fans for air circulation and use plastic sheeting to help retain moisture. A simple thermostat can help regulate heat sources such as heating pads or small space heaters.

DIY Substrate Preparation

Preparing your own substrate is another area where DIY methods can be incredibly beneficial. While you can purchase ready-made substrates, creating your own from materials like straw, wood chips, or coffee grounds not only saves money but also allows you to recycle waste products. The process involves pasteurizing or sterilizing these materials to make them safe for mushroom cultivation. For instance, straw can be pasteurized using hot water immersion—a technique that requires nothing more than a large pot, water, and a heat source.

Homemade Humidifiers and Hydration Systems

Maintaining the right humidity is crucial for mushroom cultivation, especially indoors. While commercial humidifiers are an option, you can create a simple humidification system using a plastic container, some water, and an ultrasonic fogger. These devices are often used in terrariums and are available at many pet supply stores. By placing the fogger in water within your growth chamber, you can create the necessary humid environment mushrooms thrive in.

For watering, mushrooms require a fine mist that doesn't disrupt the mycelium. A DIY misting system can be rigged from a spray bottle attached to a timer or even from repurposed perfume sprayers. This method provides a gentle shower that keeps the substrate moist without over-saturating it.

Repurposing Items for Containers

When it comes to containers, almost any clean, food-safe plastic or wood container can be adapted for growing mushrooms. Old buckets, jars, and even discarded drawers or wooden crates can be used. The primary requirements are that they hold the substrate and allow for some air exchange. Drilling holes in these containers or cutting larger openings and covering them with breathable fabric can create an ideal environment for mushroom fruiting.

Crafting Tools for Harvesting and Processing

Even harvesting and processing mushrooms can benefit from a DIY approach. A simple kitchen knife may suffice for cutting mushrooms, but creating a handle from scrap wood for a repurposed blade can make the tool more ergonomic and suited to your specific needs. Additionally, building a drying rack for mushrooms can be as simple as stretching some fabric or mesh over a frame made from scrap wood or even an old window frame.

The Advantages of DIY in Mushroom Cultivation

The benefits of taking a DIY approach to mushroom cultivation extend beyond cost savings. By building and adapting your own tools and equipment, you gain a deeper understanding of the requirements and processes involved in mushroom growth. This hands-on knowledge can be invaluable, particularly when troubleshooting issues or optimizing your setup for better yields.

Moreover, the skills you develop through DIY projects are transferable to other areas of gardening, home improvement, and even mechanical repairs. The creativity and problem-solving mindset nurtured by DIY activities are universally beneficial.

Lastly, there's an undeniable satisfaction in seeing a project through from conception to completion. The tools and equipment you craft are not just functional; they're a testament to your dedication and ingenuity in pursuing mushroom cultivation. This personal investment can make the experience all the more rewarding.

Embracing a DIY Ethic

Adopting a DIY ethic in mushroom cultivation means embracing a philosophy of learning, adaptability, and sustainability. It's about taking control of your cultivation journey, customizing it to fit your needs, and respecting the resources you have at your disposal. Whether you're a novice grower or have years of experience, the DIY route offers opportunities to innovate and economize, making mushroom cultivation accessible and enjoyable for everyone.

CHAPTER 5: THE SCIENCE OF MYCOLOGY

Mycology is not just about identifying different types of fungi; it involves understanding their life cycles, reproductive strategies, and roles within the ecosystem. This knowledge is crucial for anyone looking to cultivate mushrooms successfully, as it affects every decision from choosing the right substrate to troubleshooting common growth issues.

Here, you'll learn about the structure of fungi, starting with the basics of spores and mycelium, the true vegetative part of fungi, often unseen beneath the soil or within decaying wood. We'll also explore how these elements interact with their environment to bring forth the fruiting bodies we recognize as mushrooms. Understanding these relationships and cycles will not only enhance your ability to grow mushrooms but also deepen your appreciation for these remarkable organisms.

The chapter goes beyond the biological functions and into the practical applications of this knowledge in your cultivation efforts. From the ideal conditions that different mushrooms need to thrive to the ways you can manipulate environments to encourage growth, the science of mycology is presented as an indispensable tool for any serious cultivator.

By integrating scientific principles with practical advice, this chapter aims to equip you with the knowledge necessary to navigate the complexities of mushroom cultivation. Whether you're a novice just starting out or a seasoned grower looking to refine your techniques, understanding the underlying science of mycology is key to cultivating not just mushrooms, but a lifelong passion for these extraordinary organisms. Let's embark on this educational journey together, enhancing our practices through the profound insights that science provides.

UNDERSTANDING MYCELIUM AND SUBSTRATES

In the realm of mushroom cultivation, understanding the relationship between mycelium and substrates is essential. This knowledge not only enables you to create optimal growing conditions but also unveils the remarkable ways in which fungi interact with their environment. Let's delve into the intricate world of mycelium, the substrates they thrive on, and why this matters to you as a cultivator.

Mycelium: The Fungal Network

Mycelium refers to the dense network of thread-like structures, known as hyphae, that form the main body of a fungus. Often hidden from view beneath the soil or within decaying organic matter, this is where the real action happens. Mycelium is responsible for the absorption of nutrients and water, crucial for the fungus's growth and survival. Unlike plants, mushrooms do not photosynthesize; they rely entirely on their mycelial networks to source nutrition from the organic material around them.

The mycelium is a dynamic and responsive entity. It can sense changes in its environment and adjust its growth patterns accordingly. When conditions are favorable, it expands rapidly. If nutrients are scarce or environmental conditions become adverse, it can enter a dormant state. Understanding these behaviors is key to effective mushroom cultivation, as it influences everything from the choice of substrate to the timing of harvests.

Substrates: More Than Just Soil

The substrate in mushroom cultivation serves as the nourishment-rich bed where mycelium grows. Each type of mushroom has specific substrate preferences, typically based on what they would naturally decompose in the wild. Common substrates include:

- **Straw:** Ideal for oyster mushrooms, straw is easily colonizable due to its structure which allows the mycelium to spread quickly.

- **Wood Chips or Logs:** Used for wood-loving species like shiitake or rishi, these substrates mimic the natural environment where these mushrooms thrive.

- **Compost:** A nutrient-rich option that supports the growth of species like button mushrooms. Compost provides a complex array of nutrients that closely resembles what some mushrooms would find in their natural habitats.

- **Sawdust:** Often used in block form, sawdust can be enriched with other nutrients to grow a variety of mushrooms. It's especially popular for more commercial operations due to its consistency and ease of handling.

Choosing the right substrate is crucial as it directly impacts the health and productivity of the mycelium. Each substrate must be prepared properly to maximize its effectiveness—typically through pasteurization or sterilization to kill any unwanted bacteria or mold spores.

The Symbiosis of Mycelium and Substrate

The relationship between mycelium and its substrate is symbiotic. The substrate offers the mycelium necessary nutrients and a protective environment to grow, while the mycelium breaks down the organic material, converting it back into soil that supports other forms of life. This process is crucial for nutrient cycling in ecosystems and can be harnessed in controlled environments to both dispose of organic waste and produce food.

For cultivators, this means that maintaining the health of the mycelium is about more than just ensuring your mushrooms grow. It's about creating a mini-ecosystem where the mycelium can perform its natural roles effectively. This involves regular monitoring and adjusting conditions to prevent contamination, ensure adequate moisture and nutrient levels, and manage temperature to mimic natural growth conditions as closely as possible.

Practical Tips for Managing Mycelium and Substrates

1. **Moisture Management:** Mycelium requires moisture to grow but too much can lead to bacterial growth and mold. Maintaining a balance is critical, and using techniques like misting can help manage moisture levels without oversaturating the substrate.

2. **Temperature Control:** Different species of mushrooms thrive at different temperatures. Managing the temperature of your growing

environment can speed up or slow down mycelial growth, affecting overall yield and health.

3. **Avoiding Contamination:** Since substrates are rich in organic material, they can attract other fungi and bacteria. Keeping your growing area clean, and your substrate properly prepared, is vital to prevent contamination that can harm or kill the mycelium.

4. **Observation:** Regularly checking the development of the mycelium can provide insights into the health of your mushrooms. Healthy mycelium is typically white and spreads evenly across the substrate. Any signs of discoloration or uneven growth patterns can be early indicators of problems.

Understanding and managing the intricate relationship between mycelium and substrates is both a science and an art. It requires a blend of technical knowledge, practical skills, and attentive care. By mastering this aspect of mushroom cultivation, you not only improve your chances of a successful harvest but also deepen your connection to the fascinating life processes of fungi. This deep understanding is what transforms a novice grower into a skilled mycologist, capable of nurturing mushrooms from spore to harvest.

THE ROLE OF STERILIZATION AND PASTEURIZATION

In the meticulous world of mushroom cultivation, understanding and implementing the processes of sterilization and pasteurization are fundamental. These practices are not only about maintaining cleanliness; they're about creating a controlled environment where mushrooms can thrive without competition or threat from contaminating organisms. This sub-chapter explores why sterilization and pasteurization are crucial, how they differ, and how you can effectively use these methods in your cultivation endeavors.

Sterilization: A Clean Slate for Growth

Sterilization involves completely eliminating all forms of microbial life, including spores, bacteria, and fungi, from your cultivation environment, especially the substrate and any tools used. The most common method of sterilization in mushroom cultivation is the use of steam or pressure, typically achieved with a pressure cooker or autoclave.

Why Sterilize? Sterilization is particularly critical when working with grain spawn or any substrate that is highly nutritious and susceptible to contamination. These substrates can be breeding grounds for unwanted bacteria and molds if not properly sterilized. By removing all potential competitors, sterilization provides a blank canvas, allowing only the mushroom mycelium you introduce to flourish.

Methods and Equipment

- **Pressure Cooking:** Small to medium batches of substrate or instruments can be sterilized in a pressure cooker. This method uses steam under pressure to reach temperatures high enough to destroy all microbes.

- **Autoclaving:** For larger operations, an autoclave, which operates on a similar principle but on a larger scale, can be used.

Pasteurization: Selective Sterilization

Unlike sterilization, pasteurization does not kill all microorganisms. Instead, it reduces microbial populations to levels that won't interfere with the growth of mushroom mycelium. Pasteurization is especially useful for bulk substrates like straw or wood chips, which benefit from retaining some of their natural microbial flora to outcompete other, more harmful bacteria and molds.

Why Pasteurize? Pasteurization is key when you want to balance control with natural processes. Some beneficial microbes survive pasteurization, which can help prevent the colonization of harmful bacteria and molds by outcompeting them. This is less energy-intensive than sterilization and often sufficient for substrates used in outdoor or larger-scale indoor cultivation.

Methods and Equipment

- **Hot Water Bath:** Substrates can be submerged in hot water (around 160-180°F) for 1 to 2 hours. This method is effective for large quantities of substrate and can be done in large pots or insulated barrels.

- **Steam Pasteurization:** Exposing substrates to steam in an enclosed environment allows for effective pasteurization without the need for submersion in water. This can be done with steam generators or even DIY setups using a kettle and a closed container.

Implementing Sterilization and Pasteurization

Choosing the Right Method:

- **Small Scale Indoor Cultivation:** If you're working in a small indoor space with high-value crops like gourmet mushrooms, sterilization is often the best choice. It minimizes the risk of contamination in a controlled environment.

- **Outdoor or Large-Scale Cultivation:** Pasteurization might be more practical and cost-effective for large-scale or outdoor projects. It reduces labor and energy costs while still providing an environment conducive to growth.

Practical Tips:

1. **Monitor Temperatures:** Whether sterilizing or pasteurizing, precise temperature control is crucial. Use thermometers to ensure that your methods are effective and reaching the necessary temperatures.

2. **Time Your Processes:** Both sterilization and pasteurization require specific timeframes to be effective. Ensure that substrates are exposed to heat or steam long enough to achieve the desired microbial reduction.

3. **Cleanliness in Handling:** Post-sterilization or pasteurization, handle substrates and instruments with care. Use gloves and clean tools to avoid reintroducing contaminants.

4. **Test and Adjust:** If you encounter contamination issues, reassess your methods. Sometimes increasing the temperature slightly or extending the time can improve results.

Conclusion

Sterilization and pasteurization are not just about killing microbes; they're about fostering an environment where your chosen fungi can succeed. By understanding and applying these techniques appropriately, you can greatly enhance the reliability and yield of your mushroom cultivation efforts. This mastery of the microbial environment forms the backbone of successful mycological agriculture, ensuring that your mushrooms can grow prolifically and healthily.

CHAPTER 6: FROM SPORE TO HARVEST

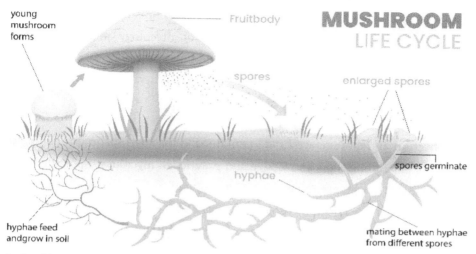

young mushroom forms

Fruitbody

MUSHROOM LIFE CYCLE

spores

enlarged spores

spores germinate

hyphae

hyphae feed andgrow in soil

mating between hyphae from different spores

Embarking on the journey from spore to harvest in the cultivation of mushrooms is akin to navigating a natural, intricate dance of growth and nurturing. This chapter delves deeply into every critical phase of a mushroom's lifecycle, from the microscopic beginnings as spores to the satisfying conclusion of harvest. Each step in this process is crucial and carries its own set of challenges and rewards, making it essential for the cultivator to understand and participate actively in each stage.

Mushrooms, in their silent, steadfast growth, tell a story of transformation. This story begins with spores, often invisible to the naked eye, which must find a suitable substrate in which to germinate. As these spores develop into mycelium, an intricate network of fungal threads, they begin their quest for nutrients, spreading out beneath the surface in search of sustenance. The journey continues as conditions prompt the mycelium to give rise to fruiting bodies—the mushrooms—that emerge from the substrate, reaching towards the light.

This chapter will guide you through setting up your cultivation environment to maximize the chances of a successful crop, from the correct preparation and inoculation of substrates to the critical monitoring of environmental conditions such as humidity, temperature, and light. Understanding these factors is paramount, as they can significantly influence the development stages of your mushrooms.

We will also explore the various methods to encourage fruiting, how to recognize when mushrooms are ready to harvest, and the best practices for gathering them to ensure continued productivity. By the end of this chapter, you will be equipped with the knowledge to not only observe but also to influence the fascinating process that takes spores and turns them into a bountiful harvest of mushrooms, ready for the kitchen or market. This is where the science of mycology meets the art of cultivation—a point where patience and care yield tangible and rewarding results.

SPORE COLLECTION AND STORAGE

Spore collection and storage are fundamental skills for any mushroom cultivator interested in expanding their knowledge and practice of mycology. Spores, akin to seeds in the plant world, are the reproductive units of fungi, capable of giving rise to new fungal colonies. The ability to collect, store, and eventually germinate these spores is an invaluable part of mastering mushroom cultivation.

The Art of Spore Collection
Collecting spores is a delicate process that requires both precision and patience. It begins with selecting a mature mushroom that is ideal for spore collection. Typically, the chosen mushroom should be healthy, free of pests, and at the right stage of development, which usually means waiting until the cap has fully opened and the gills are exposed.

Methods of Spore Collection:
1. **Spore Print Method:**
   - **Procedure:** Place the mushroom cap, gills down, on a piece of paper or glass. Cover it with a bowl to protect from air currents and leave it overnight. The spores will fall out of the cap and onto the surface, creating a spore print.
   - **Advantages:** This method is simple and visually confirms the spore's viability based on the density and uniformity of the print.
   - **Uses:** Spore prints can be stored or used directly to start cultures.
2. **Direct Collection from Fruiting Bodies:**
   - **Procedure:** Using a sterile tool, scrape spores directly from beneath the cap of the mushroom.
   - **Advantages:** It allows for immediate use and reduces the risk of contamination in some cases.

- **Uses:** Best for liquid culture preparation or immediate inoculation of substrates.

Storing Spores

Proper storage of spores is critical to maintaining their viability over time. The main enemies of spore longevity are moisture, heat, and light.

Storage Conditions:

- **Temperature:** Spores should be stored in a cool, dry place. A refrigerator can be ideal, but fluctuations in temperature should be minimized.
- **Humidity:** Excess moisture can lead to premature germination or mold issues. Spores should be kept in an airtight container with a desiccant packet to absorb any moisture.
- **Light:** Spores are sensitive to light, which can degrade them over time. Storing spores in a dark container or room is essential to extend their viability.

Packaging for Storage:

- **Glass Vials:** Small glass vials with airtight lids are excellent for spore storage. They protect the spores from light and moisture and are easy to label.
- **Foil Packets:** Aluminum foil can be used to wrap spore prints or spore-laden paper, providing light protection and minimizing space.

Shelf Life:

- Spores can remain viable for several years under optimal conditions, though viability tends to decrease over time. Regular testing of spore viability, if stored long-term, is recommended to ensure successful future cultivations.

Utilizing Stored Spores

When you are ready to use your stored spores, careful handling is key to successful germination.

1. **Hydration:** Before introducing spores to a growth medium, they often need to be hydrated. This can be done by soaking them in sterile water for several hours.
2. **Sterilization of Equipment:** Any equipment used in the handling and planting of spores should be sterilized to prevent contamination.

3. **Introduction to Growth Medium:** Spores can be introduced to a variety of growth mediums depending on the desired cultivation method. These mediums must be prepared and sterilized ahead of time.

Challenges and Tips

- **Contamination:** The biggest challenge when working with spores is avoiding contamination. Use a sterile work area, and practice good hygiene.

- **Labeling:** Always label your spore collections with the date, species, and any other relevant information to help track and organize your spore library.

- **Record Keeping:** Maintain detailed records of collection methods, storage conditions, and germination results to refine techniques over time.

Understanding and mastering spore collection and storage not only enhance your cultivation repertoire but also deepen your connection to the lifecycle of mushrooms. This knowledge empowers you to preserve and propagate mushroom genetics, offering a window into the complex and rewarding world of fungal biology. Whether for personal use, sharing with fellow enthusiasts, or contributing to biodiversity, your efforts in spore collection and storage play a vital role in the broader mycological community.

INOCULATION TECHNIQUES: BEGINNER TO ADVANCED

Inoculation is the process of introducing mushroom spores or mycelium into a substrate to initiate growth. This crucial step can vary in complexity from simple methods suitable for beginners to more advanced techniques that require precise environmental control and handling. This sub-chapter will guide you through various inoculation techniques, helping you choose and master the methods that best suit your level of experience and cultivation goals.

Beginner Techniques

For those just starting out in mushroom cultivation, simplicity is key. These methods require minimal equipment and provide a forgiving introduction to growing mushrooms.

1. Spore Syringe Inoculation:

- **Description:** A spore syringe contains mushroom spores suspended in a sterile solution. This method involves injecting the spore solution directly into the substrate.
- **Process:**
    - Sterilize the needle of the syringe with a flame.
    - Cool the needle by squirting a small amount of the solution into the air.
    - Inject the solution into several points of a sterilized substrate bag or jar.
- **Advantages:** Controlled, easy to perform, and requires minimal equipment.
- **Best for:** Small-scale indoor cultivation, especially for species like oyster mushrooms and shiitake.

2. Grain Spawn to Substrate Transfer:

- **Description:** This method involves mixing grain spawn—grains that have been fully colonized by mycelium—into pasteurized or sterilized substrate.
- **Process:**
    - Prepare your substrate and allow it to cool after pasteurization or sterilization.
    - In a clean environment, mix grain spawn thoroughly with the substrate.
- **Advantages:** Effective for scaling up production; grain spawn promotes fast colonization.
- **Best for:** Beginners ready to move beyond jar cultivation to more substantial batches.

Intermediate Techniques

As you gain confidence and experience, intermediate techniques that offer greater control over contamination and efficiency become valuable.

3. Liquid Culture Inoculation:

- **Description:** Liquid culture contains mushroom mycelium suspended in a nutrient-rich liquid. It is used to inoculate grain spawn or substrates directly.

- **Process:**
  - With sterile technique, inject liquid culture into sterilized grain jars to colonize the grain with mycelium.
  - Once fully colonized, the grain can then be used as spawn to inoculate larger amounts of substrate.
- **Advantages:** Speeds up the colonization process and reduces contamination risks due to the rapid growth of mycelium.
- **Best for:** Cultivators looking to accelerate their production cycle and work with bulk substrates.

4. Plug Spawn and Dowel Inoculation for Logs:

- **Description:** Plug spawn are small wooden dowels colonized by mycelium, used for inoculating wood logs.
- **Process:**
  - Drill holes into pasteurized logs and hammer the plug spawn into the holes.
  - Seal the holes with wax to protect from contaminants and retain moisture.
- **Advantages:** Natural method that mimics the wild environment, ideal for shiitake and other wood-loving mushrooms.
- **Best for:** Outdoor cultivators interested in a sustainable, long-term yield.

Advanced Techniques

For those who have mastered the basics and have a controlled environment, advanced techniques can optimize yield and efficiency.

5. Automated Environmental Controls:

- **Description:** Using technology to control environmental factors like humidity, temperature, and CO_2 levels.
- **Process:**
  - Set up automated systems that adjust the environment based on real-time data.
  - Use these systems to maintain optimal conditions during the inoculation and colonization phases.
- **Advantages:** Maximizes yield and quality by ensuring ideal growth conditions.

- **Best for:** Advanced cultivators looking to commercialize or scientifically optimize their operations.

6. Tissue Culture Cloning:

- **Description:** A form of micropropagation that involves growing mushroom cells in a sterile, nutrient-rich agar medium to produce clones.
- **Process:**
    - Extract a small piece of tissue from a mushroom fruit body under sterile conditions.
    - Place the tissue on agar to grow new mycelium.
- **Advantages:** Produces genetically identical clones, ideal for preserving desirable traits in gourmet species.
- **Best for:** Those with access to a lab environment and a deep interest in mushroom genetics.

Each inoculation technique offers different advantages and requires varying levels of skill and equipment. By choosing the method that aligns with your experience, facilities, and cultivation goals, you can optimize your success and enjoy the rewards of growing mushrooms from spore to harvest. As your skills grow, experimenting with more advanced techniques can further enhance your cultivation, leading to greater yields and more profound insights into the fascinating world of fungi.

THE INCUBATION AND FRUITING PHASES

Navigating the incubation and fruiting phases of mushroom cultivation is both an art and a science, requiring careful attention to detail and an understanding of the biological processes at play. These two phases are critical in determining the success of your mushroom cultivation, as they directly influence both the quality and quantity of your harvest.

The Incubation Phase

Incubation is the period during which mycelium colonizes the substrate. This phase is crucial because it sets the foundation for successful fruiting. The primary goal during incubation is to provide optimal conditions for mycelial growth, which include temperature, humidity, and cleanliness to prevent contamination.

Optimal Conditions:

- **Temperature:** Most mushrooms require specific temperature ranges during incubation that are typically lower than those for fruiting. For example, oyster mushrooms thrive at around 75-85°F during colonization.
- **Humidity:** While the substrate itself should be moist, high air humidity isn't necessary during this phase. The substrate's moisture content is more critical, as it supports mycelial growth without promoting the growth of competing molds.
- **Darkness:** Light is not required for mycelium growth and can even be detrimental during this phase, so incubating in darkness or very low light is ideal.

Monitoring and Managing the Environment:

- Regularly check the substrate for signs of healthy mycelium, which appears as white, thread-like growths. Be vigilant for any signs of mold or foul odor, which indicate contamination.
- Keep the environment stable. Fluctuations in temperature and humidity can stress the mycelium, slowing growth or leading to poor yields.

Transitioning to the Fruiting Phase

The transition from incubation to fruiting is triggered by changes in environmental conditions, often signaled by the mycelium having fully colonized the substrate. This stage requires a shift in conditions to encourage the mushrooms to form fruiting bodies.

Triggering Fruiting:

- **Introduction of Light:** Contrary to the incubation phase, light, particularly natural light or a blue LED, stimulates mushroom development.
- **Temperature Change:** A drop in temperature often signals the mycelium that it's time to fruit. For instance, reducing the temperature by 5-10 degrees can be effective.
- **Increased Air Exchange:** Higher oxygen levels are crucial for fruiting. This can be achieved by opening incubation containers or using a fan to increase air circulation.
- **Humidity:** This is the time to raise humidity levels, aiming for 85-95%, to prevent the delicate mushroom tissues from drying out.

Managing the Fruiting Phase

Once fruiting has been initiated, your role shifts to maintaining the conditions that support the growth and development of mushroom fruit bodies. This involves:

Daily Monitoring:

- Check for adequate moisture and mist the mushrooms if the environment appears dry. However, avoid direct watering of the mushrooms, as excessive moisture can damage them.
- Ensure that air circulation is sufficient to prevent CO_2 buildup, which can lead to poorly developed mushrooms.

Harvest Timing:

- Mushrooms should be harvested at the right time for the best quality. This is typically just before the veil beneath the mushroom cap breaks.
- Harvest by gently twisting the mushroom at the base to avoid damaging the mycelium, ensuring further fruiting cycles.

Post-Harvest Care:

- After each harvest, it's crucial to assess the substrate and environmental conditions to prepare for subsequent fruiting flushes.
- Substrate moisture may need replenishing, and partial re-sterilization or cleaning of the growing area might be necessary to maintain hygiene and productivity.

Understanding and carefully managing the incubation and fruiting phases are essential for a successful mushroom cultivation operation. Each step and transition require observation, adjustment, and sometimes, intervention, to create the ideal conditions for mushroom growth. With practice, these phases become less daunting and more intuitive, allowing you to produce bountiful and consistent harvests. Through this detailed engagement, cultivators not only grow mushrooms but also deepen their connection to the fascinating life cycle of fungi, enhancing both their skill and their appreciation for this unique form of agriculture.

68

CHAPTER 7: TROUBLESHOOTING AND SOLUTIONS

MUSHROOMS

Lorem ipsum dolor sit amet, consectetur. Ut porttitor nulla vel ultricies laoreet. Aenean neque. Duis accumsan erat. Curabitur suscipit dolor lectus, eu rhoncus nisl. Integer sodales accumsan.

CONTACT US   LEARN MORE

MUSHROOMS INFOGRAPHICS

Curabitur suscipit dolor lectus, eu rhoncus nisl. Integer sodales accumsan.

Lorem ipsum dolr sit amet   Lorem ipsum dolr sit amet   Lorem ipsum dolr sit amet   Lorem ipsum dolr sit amet   Lorem ipsum dolr sit amet

As you journey deeper into the world of mushroom cultivation, encountering challenges along the way is inevitable. Whether you're a novice discovering the nuances of nurturing fungi for the first time, or an experienced cultivator facing unexpected hurdles, every grower must be prepared to adapt and troubleshoot. This chapter, "Troubleshooting and Solutions," is designed as a comprehensive guide to help you navigate through common issues that may arise during the cultivation process, ensuring that your efforts result in success rather than disappointment.

Growing mushrooms involves a delicate balance of environment, care, and sometimes, a bit of luck. Issues like contamination, improper moisture levels, inadequate ventilation, or nutrient deficiencies can all throw a wrench into the works, hindering your mushrooms' growth or even ruining a batch completely. Here, we'll delve into these common problems, providing you with practical, easy-to-implement solutions.

We'll explore how to identify signs of trouble early on, such as discoloration, stunted growth, or unusual smells, which can all indicate underlying issues. Understanding what these signs mean is crucial in taking timely action to mitigate damage. Additionally, this chapter will equip you with strategies to prevent these problems from reoccurring, turning each challenge into a learning opportunity that strengthens your cultivation practice.

Through detailed explanations and guided advice, this chapter will serve not just to solve immediate cultivation issues but also to enhance your overall understanding of mushroom biology. By the end of this section, you'll not only have a toolkit of solutions for common problems but also a deeper insight into how mushrooms interact with their environment, making you a more skilled and resilient cultivator. Let's turn those cultivation challenges into opportunities for growth and improvement, ensuring that your mushroom cultivation journey is as rewarding as it is enlightening.

COMMON MISTAKES AND HOW TO AVOID THEM

Navigating the world of mushroom cultivation can be as challenging as it is rewarding. While the allure of growing your own mushrooms is strong, certain common mistakes can make the process more daunting and less productive. Understanding these pitfalls and knowing how to avoid them will not only save you time and frustration but also enhance your success and enjoyment of mushroom cultivation.

Overcomplicating the Process

Mistake: Beginners often dive into complex cultivation methods without mastering the basics, leading to frustration and failure.

Solution: Start simple. Choose easy-to-grow species like oyster mushrooms that require minimal setup and maintenance. Familiarize yourself with the basic requirements of light, temperature, and humidity before moving on to more demanding species or techniques.

Inadequate Sterilization and Pasteurization

Mistake: Neglecting proper sterilization or pasteurization of substrates and equipment, which leads to contamination.

Solution: Always adhere to recommended procedures for sterilizing and pasteurizing your substrates and tools. Invest in a good pressure cooker for sterilization and learn the correct temperatures and durations required for effectively treating your chosen substrates.

Poor Moisture Control

Mistake: Either overwatering or under-watering substrates, both of which can severely affect mycelium growth.

Solution: Maintain a balance. Mushrooms need a moist environment, but too much moisture can lead to mold and bacteria growth. Use a spray bottle for gentle misting and check your substrate's moisture levels regularly— it should feel like a wrung-out sponge.

Ignoring Environmental Controls

Mistake: Failing to control environmental factors such as temperature, humidity, and air exchange, which are critical for mushroom development.

Solution: Create a controlled growing environment. Use a thermometer and hygrometer to monitor temperature and humidity and make adjustments as necessary. Ensure there is enough ventilation to provide fresh air while keeping contaminants out.

Choosing the Wrong Substrate

Mistake: Using an inappropriate or low-quality substrate that doesn't support the growth of the chosen mushroom species.

Solution: Research and select the right substrate for your mushroom type. For example, use straw for oyster mushrooms and hardwood chips for shiitake mushrooms. Ensure your substrate is fresh, clean, and free of contaminants before use.

Overlooking the Importance of Light

Mistake: Providing too much or too little light, or using the wrong kind of light.

Solution: Understand the specific light requirements of your mushroom species. Most mushrooms require indirect light or periods of darkness to trigger fruiting. Natural light is often sufficient, but some indoor setups may benefit from supplemental LED lights.

Mismanaging Harvest Times

Mistake: Harvesting either too early or too late, which can affect both yield and quality.

Solution: Learn to recognize the signs of mature mushrooms ready for harvest. Typically, mushrooms should be harvested just before or as their veils begin to break. Regular observation and knowledge of your mushroom's growth cycle are key.

Neglecting Record Keeping

Mistake: Not maintaining records of cultivation conditions and outcomes, which can hinder your ability to repeat successes or understand failures.

Solution: Keep a cultivation journal. Record details like substrate type, inoculation date, environmental conditions, and any issues or successes. This documentation will be invaluable for troubleshooting problems and refining your techniques over time.

Avoiding Research and Learning

Mistake: Relying on trial and error without seeking out knowledge or resources that could prevent common mistakes.

Solution: Invest time in learning from books, experienced cultivators, and credible online resources. Attend workshops and join mycology clubs to gain insights and advice from the community.

By addressing these common mistakes directly and applying thoughtful solutions, you set the stage for a more fruitful and enjoyable mushroom cultivation experience. Each challenge presents an opportunity to learn and improve, and each success builds your confidence and skills as a cultivator. Remember, mushroom cultivation is not just about producing food or products; it's about cultivating patience, knowledge, and respect for nature's processes.

WHAT TO DO WHEN THINGS GO WRONG

In the journey of mushroom cultivation, even with the best plans and practices, things can sometimes veer off course. Recognizing and responding effectively when things go wrong is not only essential for salvaging your current crop but also for preventing similar issues in future cycles. This sub-chapter provides a guide on what to do when you encounter common problems in mushroom cultivation, offering practical steps to diagnose, correct, and learn from these occurrences.

Identifying the Problem

The first step in addressing any issue is accurately identifying what has gone wrong. Common problems include contamination, poor mycelium growth, lack of fruiting, or deformed mushrooms.

- **Contamination** is often visible as unusual colors or textures on your substrate or mushrooms, such as green, black, or pink patches, which indicate mold.

- **Poor mycelium growth** can be due to a variety of factors, including inadequate temperature, incorrect moisture levels, or poor-quality substrate.
- **Lack of fruiting** might result from insufficient light, incorrect humidity, or exhausted substrate.
- **Deformed mushrooms** could arise from excessive CO_2, improper lighting, or pest interference.

Immediate Actions

Once you've pinpointed the issue, taking immediate corrective actions can sometimes save a crop or prevent further losses:

- **For contamination**: Remove the contaminated parts of the substrate or entire batches, if necessary, to prevent the spread of mold or bacteria. Assess and improve your sterilization and sanitation procedures to avoid future occurrences.
- **For poor mycelium growth**: Check and adjust environmental conditions such as temperature and humidity. Ensure that the substrate is not too wet or dry by adjusting your watering practices.
- **For lack of fruiting**: Verify that all conditions for inducing fruiting have been met, including adequate light exposure, drop in temperature (if required), and sufficient air exchange. Adjust as necessary.
- **For deformed mushrooms**: Improve ventilation to reduce CO_2 levels and adjust light exposure to ensure it is adequate but not excessive.

Diagnosing Underlying Issues

If immediate actions do not resolve the issues, further investigation into the underlying causes is necessary:

- **Reevaluate your substrate**: Make sure that the substrate used is appropriate for the type of mushrooms you are growing, and that it was prepared correctly.
- **Check for equipment failure**: Sometimes issues like a broken thermostat, humidifier, or ventilation fan can disrupt the growing environment. Regular maintenance checks can prevent these occurrences.
- **Review your cultivation records**: Look back over your notes to see if there have been any deviations from previous successful grows or if a new problem has started to appear consistently.

Learning and Adjusting

Every challenge in mushroom cultivation is an opportunity to learn and refine your techniques:

- **Update your practices**: Based on what you have learned from your troubleshooting, make adjustments to your cultivation practices. This might involve changes in the sourcing of materials, updates to your environmental control setups, or modifications to your sterilization processes.

- **Educate yourself further**: Sometimes consulting more detailed texts on mycology, attending workshops, or participating in forums can provide insights that help solve more complex issues.

- **Experiment with solutions**: In cases where the solution is not straightforward, experimenting with different approaches can be beneficial. For example, trying different substrates or adjusting the timing of environmental changes during the fruiting phase can yield valuable insights.

Preventative Measures

Finally, incorporating preventative measures can help mitigate the recurrence of problems:

- **Routine checks**: Regularly inspect your mushrooms and substrate for early signs of issues. Early detection makes problems much easier to manage.

- **Improve hygiene**: Continually improving the cleanliness of your cultivation area and practices can drastically reduce contamination risks.

- **Maintain detailed records**: Keeping detailed records of every grow, including what went right and what went wrong, helps build a knowledge base that can prevent future issues.

By adopting a systematic approach to troubleshooting—identifying problems, taking corrective action, diagnosing underlying issues, and learning from each experience—you can continually improve your mushroom cultivation practice. Remember, resilience in the face of challenges is what transforms a novice into an expert. Each setback is packed with lessons, making you not just a better cultivator but also a more attuned observer of the natural world.

CHAPTER 8: ADVANCED TECHNIQUES

As you grow more confident in the foundational practices of mushroom cultivation, venturing into more sophisticated techniques can unlock new potentials and challenges. The journey from basic to advanced cultivation is marked not only by an increase in skill but also by a deeper engagement with the subtleties of mycology. This chapter, "Advanced Techniques," is designed to transition you from the essentials of mushroom growing into the realms where precision, science, and experience converge to expand both your capabilities and your cultivation horizons.

Advanced cultivation techniques offer the opportunity to increase yield, improve efficiency, and perhaps most intriguingly, enhance the quality and varieties of mushrooms you can produce. These methods are not merely about growing more mushrooms; they are about cultivating a more profound understanding of fungi and their intricate life cycles. Here, you will learn about grain-to-grain transfers, liquid cultures, and the use of automated systems that help you maintain perfect growing conditions.

We will explore sophisticated methods like creating master cultures that can be stored and used to inoculate new batches, reducing your dependency on commercial spawn. Techniques such as outdoor log cultivation, which requires patience and precise timing, will also be covered, offering you ways to expand your growing operations into natural settings.

This chapter will provide you with the knowledge to not only apply these advanced techniques but also to innovate and adapt them to your own unique cultivation environment. Whether you aim to scale up your production for commercial purposes or deepen your engagement with this fascinating hobby, the skills you develop here will serve as invaluable tools in your mycological toolkit.

By embracing these advanced techniques, you'll open up a new chapter in your cultivation journey—one that brings with it the rewards of mastery and the pleasure of discovering just how much more there is to learn about the remarkable world of mushrooms.

GRAIN-TO-GRAIN TRANSFERS

Grain-to-grain (G2G) transfers are a cornerstone advanced technique in mushroom cultivation, enabling cultivators to expand their production significantly without a proportional increase in cost or resources. This method involves transferring mycelium from a fully colonized grain jar to fresh, sterile grain jars. By mastering G2G transfers, you can efficiently scale up your operations, maintain genetic consistency, and accelerate the colonization process.

Understanding Grain-to-Grain Transfers

At its core, G2G transfer is about spreading the success of one colonized grain to initiate others. This technique mimics the natural process of mycelium expanding through the substrate but does so under controlled conditions to avoid contamination and enhance growth efficiency.

Benefits of Grain-to-Grain Transfers

1. **Cost-Effectiveness:** Reduces the need for frequent purchases of new spawn.
2. **Speed:** Accelerates the colonization of new substrates since mycelium from an already colonized grain is more robust and quicker to establish than spores.
3. **Scale:** Allows for rapid expansion of production volume without starting from spores each time.
4. **Consistency:** Maintains genetic uniformity across batches, ensuring predictable growth and fruiting characteristics.

Step-by-Step Guide to Performing a G2G Transfer

Preparation:

- **Sterilize your grains:** Before starting the transfer, ensure that your target grains are properly sterilized. Common grains used include rye, wheat, or millet due to their excellent nutrient content and structure that supports mycelial growth.

- **Prepare a sterile workspace:** Cleanliness cannot be overstated in G2G transfers. Use a laminar flow hood if available, or a still air box as an alternative. Disinfect all surfaces and tools with alcohol, and wear gloves and a face mask to minimize contamination risk.

Transfer Process:

1. **Cool the colonized grain jar:** After sterilization, allow the colonized grain jar to cool if it was recently autoclaved. This prevents thermal injury to the mycelium.

2. **Shake the colonized grain jar:** Before opening, shake the jar to loosen the grains and distribute the mycelium evenly. This step is crucial for ease of transfer.

3. **Open the jars inside the sterile workspace:** Carefully open the colonized grain jar and the sterile grain jars in your prepared workspace to avoid exposure to contaminants.

4. **Transfer the grains:** Using a sterilized spoon or similar instrument, scoop some of the colonized grains and quickly, but carefully, transfer them to your new, sterile grain jars. Aim to transfer about 10% of the colonized grains to each new jar.

5. **Seal and shake the new jars:** Seal the jars with their original lids equipped with a filter for gas exchange. Shake the jars to distribute the colonized grains throughout the sterile grains.

6. **Incubate:** Store the newly inoculated jars in an appropriate environment to encourage colonization. Monitor the jars for signs of healthy mycelium growth and any potential contamination.

Troubleshooting Common Issues

- **Contamination:** The most common issue in G2G transfers is contamination, typically from improper sterilization or aseptic technique. Always prioritize a sterile environment and handle materials as little as possible.

- **Slow colonization:** If grains are not colonizing at the expected rate, consider factors such as moisture content of the grains, incubation temperature, and the health of the mycelium being transferred.

Tips for Success

- **Use healthy and vigorous mycelium:** Select your best-performing colonized jar for transfers to ensure robust growth in subsequent jars.
- **Limit jar opening time:** Keep the time that jars are open to the air as brief as possible to minimize contamination risk.
- **Regularly refresh your master culture:** Even though G2G can be repeated many times, periodically refresh your culture from a master spore or culture to maintain vigor.

Grain-to-grain transfers are a powerful tool in the advanced cultivator's toolkit, enabling efficient scalability and robust production cycles. With practice and attention to detail, this technique can dramatically increase your output, making it a favorite among those looking to elevate their mushroom cultivation from a hobby to a more serious endeavor.

LIQUID CULTURE INOCULATION

Liquid culture inoculation is a refined technique that allows mushroom cultivators to accelerate and scale up their production with remarkable efficiency. Unlike spore inoculation, which can be somewhat unpredictable and slower, liquid culture inoculation involves introducing a nutrient-rich liquid containing pre-grown mushroom mycelium directly into the growth substrate. This method ensures a faster colonization because the mycelium is already established and merely needs to expand into the new substrate.

Understanding Liquid Culture

Liquid culture consists of a sterile nutrient solution, typically a mixture of water, sugars (like dextrose or malt extract), and sometimes other growth enhancers, in which mushroom mycelium is cultivated until it forms a dense web. This living solution can then be used to inoculate substrates directly, bypassing some of the early growth stages required from spores.

Advantages of Liquid Culture Inoculation

- **Speed:** Because the mycelium is already active and growing, it colonizes substrates more quickly than spores.
- **Economy:** A small volume of liquid culture can inoculate a large amount of substrate, making it cost-effective.

- **Scalability:** Liquid culture can be easily expanded by transferring mycelium into more nutrient solution, facilitating large-scale production without the need for continuous spore germination.
- **Reduced Contamination Risk:** The use of liquid culture in a closed system (such as injection through a self-healing port) reduces exposure to contaminants compared to more open methods.

Preparing Liquid Culture

1. **Selecting a Container:** Typically, liquid cultures are prepared in glass jars or flasks that can be sterilized. They should have airtight lids equipped with a filter for gas exchange.
2. **Sterilization:** The nutrient solution and container must be sterilized to prevent contamination. This is usually done using a pressure cooker.
3. **Inoculation of the Culture:** After cooling, the sterile nutrient solution is inoculated with mushroom mycelium, either from a spore syringe, a piece of colonized grain, or a tissue sample from a fruit body. This step should be performed under sterile conditions, often in a laminar flow hood or still air box.
4. **Incubation:** The inoculated jars are placed in a dark, warm place where the mycelium can grow throughout the liquid.

Using Liquid Culture for Inoculation

Once the liquid culture is fully colonized, it's ready to inoculate your chosen substrate:

1. **Preparation of Substrate:** Ensure that your substrate is properly pasteurized or sterilized and cooled before inoculation.
2. **Inoculation:** Using a sterile syringe or pipette, draw the mycelium-rich liquid from the culture jar. Inject the liquid culture into the substrate bags or jars through injection ports or in a sterile environment to avoid introducing contaminants.
3. **Mixing:** If the substrate is in a bag, gently mix it to distribute the mycelium evenly throughout the substrate.
4. **Incubation:** Place the inoculated substrate in conditions favorable for growth. Monitor the substrate for colonization and signs of contamination.

Troubleshooting Common Issues

- **Contamination:** If contaminants appear in your liquid culture or after inoculation, assess your sterilization and inoculation techniques. Ensure that all equipment is sterile and that the air quality during inoculation is controlled.

- **Poor Mycelium Growth:** If the mycelium seems sluggish or doesn't grow, consider the age of the culture, the quality of the nutrient solution, or the incubation conditions. Adjust as necessary for optimal growth.

Tips for Success

- **Keep Good Records:** Track batches of liquid culture with notes on recipes, growth rates, and success rates to refine your process.

- **Be Patient:** Allow the mycelium to fully colonize the liquid culture before using it for inoculation to ensure robust growth.

- **Use Quality Ingredients:** The purity of water and the quality of sugars and nutrients can affect the vitality of the mycelium.

Liquid culture inoculation represents a significant step forward in mushroom cultivation technology. It maximizes efficiency and scalability while maintaining high standards of purity and productivity. For those looking to advance their cultivation practices, mastering liquid culture techniques is an invaluable skill that opens up new possibilities in the fascinating world of mycology.

BULK GROWS FOR LARGER YIELDS

Embarking on bulk mushroom cultivation is a thrilling step for any grower seeking to maximize yield and perhaps turn a passionate hobby into a fruitful venture. Bulk growing involves scaling up production by increasing the volume of substrate and, accordingly, the output of mushrooms. This advanced technique can be highly rewarding, but it requires a solid grasp of cultivation fundamentals, meticulous planning, and precise execution.

Understanding Bulk Cultivation

Bulk cultivation refers to the process of growing mushrooms on a larger scale than typical small home setups. This method typically utilizes extensive amounts of substrate, larger growing containers or beds, and, often, more sophisticated environmental control systems. The goal is to produce enough mushrooms to meet higher demand—whether for commercial sale, large-scale culinary use, or community distribution.

Setting Up for Bulk Grows

The transition from smaller grows to bulk cultivation requires careful consideration of several factors:

1. **Choice of Substrate:** The type of substrate you choose must be appropriate for the mushroom species and scalable for larger grows. Common bulk substrates include straw for oyster mushrooms and supplemented sawdust for shiitake or rishi. The substrate must be prepared (usually pasteurized or sterilized) on a larger scale, which might require bigger equipment or more space.

2. **Space Requirements:** Bulk growing demands significantly more space than small-scale cultivation. Whether you're adapting a section of a barn, a basement, or a dedicated mushroom shed, ensure that your space can maintain the necessary environmental conditions.

3. **Environmental Control:** Managing temperature, humidity, and fresh air exchange becomes more complex as the scale increases. Automated systems for heating, cooling, and humidifying can help maintain the ideal environment and are often necessary for consistent production.

4. **Inoculation and Colonization:** Inoculating larger amounts of substrate requires more spawn or a more efficient method such as liquid culture inoculation. The colonization process in bulk systems must be closely monitored for any signs of contamination or uneven growth.

Process of Bulk Cultivation

Once the setup is ready, the cultivation process follows these steps:

1. **Preparation and Sterilization:** Prepare and sterilize the substrate on a large scale. This might involve using industrial-sized steamers or custom-built pasteurization tunnels.

2. **Inoculation:** Inoculate the prepared substrate with spawn. This step should be done with care to ensure even distribution of spawn throughout the substrate.

3. **Incubation:** Place the inoculated substrate in an incubation area where conditions are controlled to favor mycelial growth. This stage requires vigilance to maintain the right conditions and prevent any contamination.

4. **Initiating Fruiting:** Once the substrate is fully colonized, conditions are changed to initiate fruiting. This usually involves introducing fresh air, adjusting humidity, and exposing the substrate to more light.

5. **Maintenance During Fruiting:** During the fruiting phase, ongoing maintenance is crucial. Daily monitoring and adjustments ensure that the mushrooms have the best conditions for growth.

6. **Harvest:** Bulk grows often produce several flushes of mushrooms. Harvesting must be timely to ensure the highest quality and yield. Between flushes, conditions are maintained to support continued fruiting.

Challenges and Solutions in Bulk Grows

Scaling up to bulk production introduces new challenges, primarily related to managing larger volumes of materials and maintaining stricter control over environmental conditions.

- **Contamination Risk:** Larger amounts of substrate and longer processing times can increase the risk of contamination. Implement rigorous sterilization and hygiene practices to mitigate this risk.

- **Environmental Control:** Automated environmental control systems can help manage the complexity of maintaining ideal growing conditions across larger spaces.

- **Labor and Time Management:** Bulk growing is labor-intensive. Efficient planning and possibly additional help are crucial for managing the increased workload.

Conclusion

Bulk mushroom cultivation is an exciting progression for any grower ready to scale their operations. It offers the opportunity to significantly increase production but requires careful planning, a deeper understanding of mycology, and more advanced management techniques. With the right preparation and knowledge, bulk growing can be an immensely rewarding endeavor, providing abundant harvests and the satisfaction of mastering large-scale mushroom production.

CHAPTER 9: COMMERCIAL CULTIVATION

Transitioning from hobbyist to commercial mushroom cultivator marks a significant leap, transforming a passion into a profession. This chapter, "Commercial Cultivation," is crafted to guide you through the complexities of scaling up your mushroom cultivation to a commercial operation, blending the art of mycology with the science of business management.

As you step into the realm of commercial cultivation, you will face new challenges and opportunities that demand not only a deep understanding of mushroom cultivation but also a keen sense of business acumen. Here, we will explore the essential elements of establishing and running a successful commercial mushroom farm, from choosing the right production method and scaling operations to navigating market dynamics and customer relationships.

Commercial cultivation requires a holistic approach; it's not merely about growing a product but also about crafting a brand, understanding market needs, and developing efficient processes that maximize both yield and profits. You will learn how to design a facility that supports optimal mushroom growth, implement systems that streamline production, and adopt technologies that enhance both productivity and product quality.

Furthermore, this chapter will delve into the financial aspects of running a commercial mushroom operation, including initial investments, ongoing expenses, and revenue management. We'll also discuss the importance of marketing and sales strategies that resonate with your target audience, helping you to establish a strong presence in the market.

Whether you aim to supply local restaurants, sell at farmers' markets, or distribute on a larger scale, the journey to commercial mushroom cultivation is as rewarding as it is challenging. It invites you to not only become a master of mushroom cultivation but also to grow as an entrepreneur and innovator in the field. Let's embark on this journey together, equipping you with the knowledge and tools needed to thrive in the competitive world of commercial mushroom cultivation.

Scaling Up Your Operations

Scaling up your mushroom cultivation from a hobbyist or small-scale operation to a commercial venture is a significant transformation that requires careful planning, resource management, and strategic decision-making. This expansion isn't just about increasing the volume of your production; it involves enhancing every aspect of your operation to support larger-scale outputs and meet commercial demands effectively.

Understanding the Scope of Scaling Up

Scaling up involves several dimensions beyond just growing more mushrooms. It includes developing your facilities, optimizing your production processes, managing increased labor needs, and handling more sophisticated sales and distribution strategies. Each of these areas needs to be addressed thoughtfully and systematically to ensure a smooth transition and sustainable growth.

Facility Expansion

The first logical step in scaling up is often expanding your physical space. This might mean moving from a home setup into a larger, dedicated facility or expanding your existing space to accommodate more growing units.

- **Location Considerations:** When choosing a location for expansion, consider factors like climate control, proximity to markets, and potential for future growth. Ensuring that your new space can maintain the environmental conditions that mushrooms require is crucial.

- **Infrastructure Needs:** Larger operations may require more sophisticated infrastructure, including advanced ventilation systems, larger autoclaves or steaming equipment for substrate sterilization, and automated climate control systems.

Process Optimization

As you scale up, small inefficiencies can become costly. Streamlining your cultivation process to maximize yield and reduce waste is essential.

- **Automation:** Implementing automation in areas like watering, temperature, and humidity control can save time and reduce labor costs.

Even partial automation, such as using timers for misting systems, can significantly impact.

- **Batch Scheduling:** Optimizing your production schedule to ensure continuous output can help meet consistent market demands. This might involve staggered planting cycles or having different growing rooms at various stages of production.

Labor Management

Scaling up inevitably means you'll need more hands-on deck. Managing increased labor requirements efficiently involves several key components:

- **Hiring Skilled Workers:** As your operation grows, hiring employees with experience or training in mushroom cultivation or at least agricultural practices can improve the quality and efficiency of your production.

- **Training Programs:** Developing training programs for new employees is vital to maintain high standards. Regular training on hygiene, cultivation techniques, and safety measures is essential.

- **Roles and Responsibilities:** Clearly defined roles and responsibilities help ensure that all tasks are covered and that there's accountability in the workflow.

Financial Planning and Management

Increased scale means increased financial stakes. Careful financial planning and management become even more critical as you grow.

- **Budgeting:** Detailed budgeting for expansion costs, ongoing operational expenses, and unexpected costs is crucial. This should include everything from substrate and spawn costs to utilities and employee salaries.

- **Funding:** Securing additional funding may be necessary. This could come from reinvesting profits, taking out loans, or finding investors. Clear financial records and a solid business plan will be essential for securing investment.

Sales and Marketing

With more products to sell, enhancing your marketing and expanding your sales channels will be necessary.

- **Market Research:** Understand your target markets, what they require, and how best to reach them. This may involve everything from online marketing to attending trade shows.

- **Customer Relationships:** Build strong relationships with buyers such as local restaurants, grocery stores, and farmers' markets. Reliable customer service and consistent product quality can help secure long-term contracts.
- **Diversification:** Consider diversifying your product range to include different mushroom species or value-added products like mushroom powders or medicinal extracts.

Regulatory Compliance

Larger operations often come under closer scrutiny by regulatory bodies. Compliance with agricultural and food safety regulations is essential to avoid costly legal issues.

- **Certifications:** Obtaining organic certification or other relevant certifications can not only ensure compliance but also serve as a marketing tool.
- **Regular Inspections:** Prepare for and maintain readiness for health and safety inspections, which may occur more frequently as your operation grows.

Scaling up your mushroom cultivation operation is a dynamic and potentially rewarding endeavor that requires a holistic approach to manage increased complexity. By focusing on strategic planning in facility expansion, process optimization, labor management, financial management, and market expansion, you can build a robust business capable of thriving in the competitive commercial landscape.

MARKETING AND SELLING YOUR PRODUCE

In the realm of commercial mushroom cultivation, producing a high-quality product is only half the battle. The other half is effectively marketing and selling your mushrooms, which can be as crucial as the cultivation process itself. This sub-chapter explores the essentials of marketing and selling your mushroom produce, providing strategies to enhance visibility, engage customers, and maximize revenue.

Understanding Your Market

Before diving into sales strategies, it's vital to understand your market. This involves identifying who your buyers are, what types of mushrooms they prefer, and how much they are willing to pay. Potential markets for mushrooms include:

- **Local restaurants and chefs** who value fresh, high-quality ingredients.
- **Farmers' markets**, where consumers seek local, organic produce.
- **Grocery stores** and **specialty food shops** looking to offer unique or gourmet products.
- **Online consumers**, particularly those interested in health and wellness products.

Each market segment has different expectations and requires tailored approaches.

Branding and Positioning

Your brand is your promise to your customers. It tells them what they can expect from your products, and it differentiates your offering from your competitors'. Effective branding encompasses:

- **Logo and Packaging Design**: Professional, attractive packaging can greatly influence buying decisions. Ensure your packaging reflects the quality of your product and adheres to any labeling regulations.
- **Unique Selling Proposition (USP)**: What makes your mushrooms stand out? Perhaps it's their organic status, unique varieties, or the sustainable methods you use. Your USP should be clear in all your marketing materials.

Marketing Strategies

Effective marketing strategies can help you build brand awareness and attract more customers. Consider the following approaches:

- **Content Marketing**: Sharing engaging content related to mushrooms, such as recipes, health benefits, and cooking tips, can help attract and educate potential customers.
- **Social Media Marketing**: Platforms like Instagram, Facebook, and Twitter are excellent for visual products like mushrooms. Regular posts featuring images of your mushrooms, cultivation process, and behind-the-scenes looks can engage followers.

- **Email Marketing**: Collecting emails from customers and sending them updates about new products, offers, or mushroom seasons keeps your audience engaged.
- **Collaborations**: Partnering with local chefs, food bloggers, or wellness influencers can help introduce your products to a broader audience.

Sales Channels

Choosing the right sales channels is crucial for getting your mushrooms to the market efficiently:

- **Direct Sales**: Selling directly to consumers through farmers' markets or your own website can provide higher margins and direct customer feedback.
- **Wholesale**: Selling in bulk to restaurants, grocery stores, or distributors might offer less profit per unit but can lead to higher overall volume.
- **Subscription Boxes**: Offering a subscription service for regular deliveries of fresh mushrooms can ensure steady demand and improve customer loyalty.

Customer Relations

Maintaining excellent customer relationships is essential for long-term success. This includes:

- **Reliability**: Always deliver what you promise, in terms of both quality and quantity.
- **Customer Service**: Respond promptly and courteously to customer inquiries and complaints.
- **Feedback**: Encourage and listen to customer feedback to improve your products and services.

Pricing Strategies

Setting the right price for your mushrooms is critical. It must cover your costs, offer a competitive margin, and match the perceived value by your customers. Consider the following:

- **Cost-Plus Pricing**: Calculate the total cost of production and add a markup for profit.
- **Market-Oriented Pricing**: Set prices based on what the market can bear, considering what competitors charge and what customers are willing to pay.

- **Dynamic Pricing**: Adjust prices based on demand, availability, and seasonal changes.

Monitoring and Adapting

The market is always changing, and successful mushroom cultivators must be adept at adapting their strategies to new trends and feedback. Regularly review your sales performance, market trends, and customer preferences. Be prepared to adjust your marketing and sales strategies to stay competitive and meet changing market demands.

By embracing a comprehensive approach to marketing and selling your mushrooms, you can not only capture and grow your share of the market but also build a sustainable business model that thrives on customer satisfaction and repeat business.

ETHICAL AND SUSTAINABLE PRACTICES

In the pursuit of commercial mushroom cultivation, embracing ethical and sustainable practices is not just a moral obligation but a strategic approach that can enhance both the viability and the value of your business. As public awareness of environmental issues and corporate responsibility grows, businesses that prioritize sustainability not only contribute positively to the world but also position themselves competitively in a market that increasingly values green practices.

Understanding Ethical and Sustainable Cultivation

Ethical and sustainable cultivation involves practices that minimize environmental impact, use resources responsibly, and promote fair labor standards. For mushroom cultivators, this means managing your operation in ways that conserve water and energy, reduce waste, and ensure that all workers are treated fairly and with respect.

Key Areas of Focus

1. Resource Management

- **Water Usage**: Mushrooms require a humid environment, but excessive water use can be wasteful and costly. Implementing water recycling systems or using techniques that maximize humidity while minimizing water waste are both effective strategies.

- **Energy Efficiency**: Utilizing energy-efficient growing technologies, such as LED lighting and solar panels, can reduce your carbon footprint and lower energy costs.
- **Sustainable Materials**: Opt for renewable or recycled materials for your growing mediums and packaging. For example, using biodegradable plant-based plastics for packaging can appeal to eco-conscious consumers.

2. Waste Reduction

- **Substrate Recycling**: After harvest, used substrates can be composted and repurposed as fertilizer for other agricultural practices, reducing waste and contributing to soil health.
- **Edible By-Products**: Consider marketing smaller, less aesthetically pleasing mushrooms that might not meet the premium market standards as a separate, discounted product line or use them to create value-added products like pickled mushrooms or mushroom broths.

3. Chemical Use

- **Pesticides and Fungicides**: Avoid using chemical pesticides and fungicides. If pest control is necessary, opt for organic or natural alternatives that do not harm the environment or the health of consumers and workers.

4. Labor Practices

- **Fair Labor**: Ensure that all employees are paid fair wages and work under safe conditions. This not only adheres to ethical standards but also boosts worker satisfaction and productivity.
- **Community Engagement**: Engage with local communities by offering workshops, participating in local sustainability programs, or providing community-supported agriculture (CSA) memberships that include mushrooms.

5. Biodiversity

- **Cultivating Native Species**: Whenever possible, include native mushroom species in your cultivation plans. This supports local biodiversity and can also reduce the risk of introducing non-native species that might become invasive.

6. Certifications

- **Organic and Sustainability Certifications**: Obtaining certifications like USDA Organic or similar credentials in your region can not only assure customers of your commitment to sustainable practices but also allow you to command higher prices for your products.

Implementing Sustainable Practices

Transitioning to sustainable methods can be challenging, especially for established operations. Start by assessing the current impact of your cultivation practices and identifying areas where improvements can be made. Develop a phased plan to implement changes that manage costs while achieving sustainability goals.

Monitoring and Feedback

Regular monitoring of energy consumption, water usage, waste production, and worker conditions is essential. Use this data to continuously improve your processes. Solicit feedback from employees, customers, and local community members to enhance your practices further.

Community and Industry Engagement

Participating in industry groups and local community organizations focused on sustainability can provide valuable insights and resources. These groups offer a platform to share experiences, learn from others, and even influence regional policies on sustainable agriculture.

Benefits of Ethical and Sustainable Practices

Embracing sustainability can transform challenges into business opportunities. Benefits include:

- **Market Differentiation**: Positioning your mushrooms as sustainably grown can differentiate your product in a crowded market.

- **Customer Loyalty**: Consumers are increasingly loyal to brands that demonstrate ethical responsibility.

- **Operational Efficiencies**: Many sustainable practices lead to lower long-term operational costs.

- **Enhanced Reputation**: Being known as a sustainable business can enhance your brand's reputation, attracting more customers and skilled employees.

By integrating ethical and sustainable practices into every aspect of your mushroom cultivation business, you not only contribute to the health of the planet and its people but also build a resilient and respected brand that stands out in today's competitive market.

CHAPTER 10: HARVESTING AND STORAGE

As you stand amidst your burgeoning crop of mushrooms, the thrill of the initial planting and nurturing fades into a quieter, yet equally profound, phase of the cultivation cycle: harvesting and storage. This chapter is dedicated to that pivotal moment when the fruits of your labor are finally ready to transition from the grow room to the kitchen table—or perhaps even to market shelves.

Harvesting mushrooms isn't merely a mechanical task; it's an art form that blends timing, technique, and intuition. Each variety of mushroom sings its readiness through unique cues: a slight unfurling of the cap, a particular denseness to the touch, or a subtle shift in color. Learning to read these signs is akin to learning a new language—one spoken only within the damp and earthy confines of a mushroom farm.

This chapter aims not just to instruct but to guide you through the nuances of that language. You will learn how to determine the exact moment your mushrooms are at their peak, capturing all their flavor and nutritional value before these ephemeral delights begin their inevitable decline.

Storage, too, is more than a mere afterthought; it is an essential aspect of mushroom cultivation that demands careful consideration. Proper storage techniques can extend the shelf life of your harvest, preserving the quality of your mushrooms while maximizing their culinary and commercial value. Whether you are a home cook looking to savor your harvest over many meals, or a commercial grower aiming to deliver the best possible product to your customers, understanding how to effectively store your mushrooms is crucial.

Together, harvesting and storage form the closing chapters of your mushrooms' journey from spore to table. As we explore these processes, remember that each step taken with care and respect not only honors your hard work but also deepens your connection to the natural world. Through this chapter, let's embrace the end of one cycle and the beginning of another, each harvest bringing new insights and opportunities.

WHEN AND HOW TO HARVEST

Mushrooms, unlike the plants in your garden, don't conform to simple rules of thumb when it comes to harvesting. Each variety whispers its readiness in a language shaped by subtle signs—a language you, as a cultivator, will soon learn to interpret with ease. Let's explore the artful timing and methods that ensure you reap the fullest flavors and optimal textures from your fungal bounty.

Timing the Harvest: A Dance with Nature

The moment of harvest is a delicate balance, a dance with nature that requires a keen eye and a patient hand. For most mushroom varieties, the key indicator is the state of the mushroom cap. Typically, mushrooms are best harvested just as the veil beneath the cap begins to tear away from the stalk. This stage is not just visually striking, but crucial, as it signifies that the spores are about to be released.

In the case of **shiitake mushrooms**, watch for the cap to open fully, slightly curling at the edges, a sign that they are at peak flavor. Conversely, **oyster mushrooms** should be picked when the edges of the cap are still slightly downturned. Harvesting at this phase ensures the mushrooms are still tender and not overly fibrous.

For **button mushrooms**, consistency in size can often be a better gauge than cap position. Harvesting while the cap is still closed ensures a firm texture, ideal for culinary uses where structure is key, such as salads or as toppings.

Timing your harvest is not merely about observing the physical characteristics of your mushrooms. It's about synchronizing with their natural cycle to maximize yield and quality. Harvest too early, and you sacrifice size and potentially flavor; too late, and the mushrooms may become soggy and less palatable.

How to Harvest: Techniques That Honor Your Efforts

Harvesting mushrooms is not just about picking them; it's about how you pick them. The method can affect not only the current crop but also the health and productivity of future ones.

1. The Twist and Pull:

This method is most commonly used for mushrooms like the common button or portobello. Grasp the stem close to the ground, twist it gently, and pull. This technique helps to avoid damaging the mycelium—the complex web of filaments that gives rise to mushrooms. By preserving the mycelium, you ensure that it continues to produce future generations of mushrooms.

2. Cutting:

For varieties that are denser or grow in clusters, such as oyster mushrooms, a sharp knife may be necessary. Cut the mushrooms at the base, being careful not to disturb the substrate. This method is particularly useful when the mushrooms are tightly packed, and twisting could harm adjacent fungi.

3. The Whole-Cluster Approach:

Certain types of mushrooms, like shiitake, often grow in clusters that can be harvested in one go. Gently grasp the cluster at the base and twist it free from the substrate. This method is efficient and helps keep the mushrooms together, which is especially useful for maintaining their form and integrity if they are headed straight to the market or kitchen.

Post-Harvest Handling: Ensuring Continued Quality

Once harvested, mushrooms must be handled with care to maintain their quality. Unlike fruits and vegetables that can be washed vigorously, mushrooms absorb water readily and should therefore be cleaned gently. A soft brush or a piece of damp cloth is often all that is needed to remove any substrate particles clinging to the caps and stems.

Immediate post-harvest treatment also includes sorting the mushrooms by size and type, which facilitates uniform drying or cooking. It's advisable to use mushrooms as soon after harvesting as possible to enjoy their best texture and flavor. However, if you must store them, a paper bag in the refrigerator offers an ideal environment. The paper bag absorbs excess moisture and allows for a bit of air circulation, keeping the mushrooms dry but not dehydrated.

The Ethical Harvest: A Note on Sustainability

Harvesting mushrooms at home or on a small scale allows you to control many aspects of the cultivation process, from substrate selection to harvest method. This control can be leveraged to ensure that your mushroom cultivation is sustainable and ethical. Consider using organic substrates and avoiding chemical additives to promote a healthy ecosystem both within and beyond your cultivation area.

Moreover, think of the spent substrate as a resource rather than waste. Spent substrates, rich in organic matter, make excellent additions to compost or as soil amendments, thereby closing the loop in your cultivation practice.

Conclusion

The act of harvesting mushrooms is rich with significance. It marks the culmination of your efforts and the beginning of new cycles of growth. Each mushroom you gently twist from the earth carries with it a story of care, patience, and a deep connection to the mysterious world of fungi. By mastering the when and how of harvesting, you not only ensure the quality and yield of your crops but also deepen your relationship with the natural world. Happy harvesting!

POST-HARVEST PROCEDURES AND STORAGE

Once the meticulous work of cultivating mushrooms has culminated in a successful harvest, your focus must shift towards post-harvest procedures and storage. These crucial steps ensure that the quality of the mushrooms is preserved from the moment they are picked until they reach the consumer. Proper post-harvest handling is vital not only to maintain the mushrooms' freshness and texture but also to maximize their shelf life and nutritional value.

Immediate Post-Harvest Handling

The first few hours after harvesting are critical in determining the longevity and quality of mushrooms. Mushrooms are highly perishable, and without proper handling, they can quickly lose their optimum qualities.

- **Cooling**: Mushrooms should be cooled as quickly as possible after harvesting to slow down enzymatic reactions that lead to spoilage. Cooling to a temperature of around 2°C (35°F) within an hour of harvesting is ideal. This rapid cooling process, often referred to as 'pre-cooling,' can significantly extend the shelf life of mushrooms.
- **Cleaning**: Mushrooms should be gently cleaned to remove any substrate or debris. However, they should not be washed with water unless they are to be used immediately, as moisture can hasten spoilage. Instead, use a soft brush or cloth to lightly wipe each mushroom.
- **Sorting and Grading**: Mushrooms should be sorted and graded according to size, type, and quality. Damaged or overly mature mushrooms should be separated from premium quality mushrooms to ensure uniformity in packaging.

Packaging

Proper packaging is essential to protect mushrooms from physical damage, contamination, and moisture loss. It also plays a crucial role in maintaining the controlled environment necessary for their preservation.

- **Material**: Use packaging materials that are breathable yet capable of maintaining humidity. Materials such as perforated plastic bags or boxes lined with absorbent paper are commonly used.
- **Method**: The packaging method should minimize handling damage. Mushrooms can be packed loosely in shallow trays or boxes, which allow for some air circulation around each piece.

Storage Conditions

The storage environment should be carefully controlled to maximize the shelf life of harvested mushrooms.

- **Temperature**: The ideal storage temperature for most mushrooms is between 1°C and 4°C (34°F to 39°F). Temperatures that are too low or too high can cause damage or premature spoilage.
- **Humidity**: Maintain a high relative humidity, around 85-95%, to prevent the mushrooms from drying out. However, the environment should not be so humid that condensation forms on the mushrooms or inside the packaging, as this can promote bacterial growth.
- **Ventilation**: Good air circulation helps to remove ethylene gas and other metabolic products that can accelerate aging and spoilage.

Advanced Storage Techniques

For those looking to extend the shelf life of mushrooms beyond typical parameters, several advanced techniques can be employed:

- **Controlled Atmosphere Storage**: Adjusting the levels of oxygen, carbon dioxide, and nitrogen in the storage environment can slow down the respiration rate of mushrooms and extend their freshness.
- **Modified Atmosphere Packaging (MAP)**: This technique involves altering the atmospheric composition inside the packaging to extend shelf life. MAP often uses films that have specific permeability to gases, balancing the oxygen and carbon dioxide levels around the mushrooms.

Monitoring and Evaluation

Regular monitoring of stored mushrooms is essential to manage their quality and detect any signs of spoilage early. Key indicators to monitor include:

- **Appearance**: Check for any signs of discoloration, wilting, or slime, which indicate spoilage.
- **Odor**: Any off-smells or unusual odors can be a sign of bacterial growth or spoilage.
- **Texture**: Mushrooms that become overly soft or exhibit a rubbery texture are generally past their best quality.

Practical Tips for Handling

- **Handle with Care**: Mushrooms are delicate. Handle them as little as possible during post-harvest processes to prevent bruising.
- **Train Staff**: Ensure that all personnel involved in the handling, packaging, and storage of mushrooms are trained on the best practices and understand the importance of maintaining quality.

Proper post-harvest handling and storage are as crucial as the cultivation process itself. By implementing these procedures effectively, you can ensure that the mushrooms retain their highest quality, safety, and nutritional value, thus enhancing their marketability and extending their shelf life.

CHAPTER 11: COOKING AND ENJOYING YOUR HARVEST

As you traverse the journey from cultivator to cook, the air fills not just with the earthy scent of fresh mushrooms, but also with anticipation. Now, with baskets laden with your harvest, we turn from the garden and forest to the hearth and home, where the true alchemy of mushroom cultivation reveals itself in the kitchen. This chapter is a celebration of that transformation, from raw fungal fruit to culinary gold.

Cooking with mushrooms you've grown yourself offers an unparalleled satisfaction. Each dish prepared is not only a testament to your labor but also an exploration of flavors and textures unique to fungi. Whether it's the robust, meaty bite of a portobello or the delicate, almost seafood-like taste of oyster mushrooms, your harvest brings with it endless possibilities for culinary creativity.

Here, we'll explore how to best honor your mushrooms through cooking. We'll discuss not just how to prepare them to highlight their distinct characteristics, but also how to pair them with other ingredients to elevate simple meals into memorable feasts. From the simplest sauté to the most intricate mushroom risotto, the recipes and techniques shared in this chapter will guide you through using your harvest in ways that delight both the palate and the spirit.

Moreover, this chapter extends beyond mere recipes. It's an invitation to experience the joy of sharing your bounty. Cooking is as much about community as it is about ingredients, and mushrooms, with their complex flavors and communal nature, are particularly suited to shared meals and celebrations.

As we delve into the various ways to cook and enjoy your mushrooms, remember that each meal is a reflection of the journey you have embarked on. The flavors you create are enriched by the knowledge of where they came from and the care with which they were cultivated. Let's bring your mushrooms from soil to supper with a spirit of adventure and a celebration of flavor.

SIMPLE AND DELICIOUS MUSHROOM RECIPES

Mushrooms offer a culinary versatility that is unmatched by many other ingredients, bringing depth and earthiness to dishes that range from simple snacks to elaborate entrees. In this selection of recipes, we explore a variety of ways to cook mushrooms, each designed to highlight their unique flavors and textures. Whether you're in the mood for a comforting soup, a hearty main, or a delicate appetizer, these recipes are sure to delight any mushroom lover. From the robustness of a Portobello burger to the subtle elegance of stuffed mushrooms, there's a dish here for every occasion.

MUSHROOM SOUP WITH THYME

PREPARATION TIME: 15 min - **COOKING TIME:** 30 min
MODE OF COOKING: Simmering - **SERVINGS:** 4
INGREDIENTS:

- 1 lb. fresh mixed mushrooms (shiitake, button, and portobello), finely chopped
- 1 large onion, diced
- 2 cloves garlic, minced
- 4 cups vegetable broth
- 1 cup heavy cream
- 2 Tbsp unsalted butter
- 1 Tbsp olive oil
- 2 tsp fresh thyme leaves
- Salt and pepper to taste

DIRECTIONS:

1. In a large pot, heat butter and olive oil over medium heat.
2. Add onions and garlic, cooking until soft and translucent.
3. Stir in mushrooms and thyme, cook until mushrooms have browned and released their moisture.

4. Pour in vegetable broth and bring to a boil, then reduce to a simmer for 20 min.
5. Blend soup until smooth using an immersion blender, stir in heavy cream, and season with salt and pepper.
6. Simmer for an additional 10 min, adjust seasoning if necessary, and serve hot.

TIPS:

- For a vegan version, substitute cream with coconut milk and butter with a plant-based alternative.
- Garnish with crispy fried mushrooms for added texture.

N.V.: Calories: 210, Fat: 18g, Carbs: 12g, Protein: 4g, Sugar: 5g

PORTOBELLO MUSHROOM BURGER

PREPARATION TIME: 10 min - **COOKING TIME:** 15 min
MODE OF COOKING: Grilling - **SERVINGS:** 2
INGREDIENTS:

- 2 large Portobello mushroom caps
- 2 Tbsp balsamic vinegar
- 1 Tbsp olive oil
- 1 tsp smoked paprika
- Salt and pepper to taste
- 2 burger buns
- Lettuce, tomato slices, and red onion for serving

DIRECTIONS:

1. Clean mushroom caps with a damp cloth and remove stems.
2. In a small bowl, mix olive oil, balsamic vinegar, smoked paprika, salt, and pepper.
3. Brush both sides of mushrooms with the marinade and let sit for 10 min.
4. Preheat grill to medium-high heat (375°F / 190°C).
5. Grill mushrooms for about 7 min on each side or until tender.
6. Serve on buns with lettuce, tomato, and onion.

TIPS:

- Add a slice of cheese during the last minute of grilling for a melty touch.

- Serve with a side of sweet potato fries for a hearty meal.

N.V.: Calories: 290, Fat: 13g, Carbs: 35g, Protein: 9g, Sugar: 8g

STUFFED MUSHROOMS WITH GOAT CHEESE AND HERBS

PREPARATION TIME: 20 min - **COOKING TIME:** 20 min

MODE OF COOKING: Baking - **SERVINGS:** 4

INGREDIENTS:

- 12 large cremini mushrooms, stems removed and finely chopped
- 4 oz goat cheese, softened
- 1/4 cup breadcrumbs
- 2 Tbsp fresh parsley, chopped
- 1 Tbsp fresh chives, chopped
- 1 garlic clove, minced
- 2 Tbsp olive oil
- Salt and pepper to taste

DIRECTIONS:

1. Preheat oven to 375°F (190°C).
2. In a skillet, heat 1 Tbsp olive oil over medium heat. Sauté mushroom stems and garlic until tender.
3. In a bowl, combine sautéed stems with goat cheese, breadcrumbs, parsley, chives, salt, and pepper. Mix until well combined.
4. Stuff mushroom caps with the filling and place on a baking sheet. Drizzle with remaining olive oil.
5. Bake in the preheated oven for 20 min or until the mushrooms are tender and the tops are golden brown.

TIPS:

- For extra flavor, drizzle with a balsamic reduction before serving.
- Can be served as an appetizer or paired with a salad for a light meal.

N.V.: Calories: 180, Fat: 12g, Carbs: 10g, Protein: 7g, Sugar: 2g

MUSHROOM AND SPINACH LASAGNA

PREPARATION TIME: 25 min - **COOKING TIME:** 45 min

MODE OF COOKING: Baking - **SERVINGS:** 6

INGREDIENTS:

- 9 lasagna noodles
- 1 lb. fresh spinach, washed and chopped
- 1 lb. mixed mushrooms (shiitake, button, portobello), sliced
- 1 onion, finely chopped
- 3 cloves garlic, minced
- 15 oz ricotta
- 1 cup shredded mozzarella
- 1/2 cup grated Parmesan cheese
- 2 cups marinara sauce
- 2 Tbsp olive oil
- Salt and pepper to taste

DIRECTIONS:

1. Preheat oven to 375°F (190°C).
2. Cook lasagna noodles according to package instructions; set aside.
3. In a large skillet, heat olive oil over medium heat. Add onion and garlic, cook until translucent.
4. Add mushrooms and cook until they release their juices and become golden. Stir in spinach until wilted.
5. In a mixing bowl, combine ricotta, half the mozzarella, and salt and pepper.
6. Spread a thin layer of marinara sauce in the bottom of a baking dish. Layer noodles, ricotta mixture, mushroom and spinach mixture, and more sauce. Repeat layers, finishing with noodles and sauce.
7. Top with remaining mozzarella and Parmesan cheese.
8. Cover with foil and bake for 30 min. Remove foil and bake for another 15 min or until the top is golden and bubbly.

TIPS:

- Add a layer of cooked Italian sausage for extra flavor if desired.
- Let the lasagna sit for 10 min after baking for easier slicing.

CREAMY MUSHROOM AND CHICKEN PASTA

PREPARATION TIME: 15 min - **COOKING TIME:** 20 min

MODE OF COOKING: Sauteing - **SERVINGS:** 4

INGREDIENTS:

- 1 lb. penne pasta
- 1 lb. chicken breast, thinly sliced
- 1 lb. button mushrooms, sliced
- 1 cup heavy cream
- 1/2 cup chicken broth
- 1 onion, diced
- 2 cloves garlic, minced
- 2 Tbsp olive oil
- 1/4 cup grated Parmesan cheese
- Salt and pepper to taste
- Fresh parsley, chopped for garnish

DIRECTIONS:

1. Cook pasta according to package instructions; drain and set aside.
2. In a large skillet, heat olive oil over medium-high heat. Add chicken and season with salt and pepper. Cook until golden and cooked through. Remove from skillet and set aside.
3. In the same skillet, add more oil if needed, and sauté onions and garlic until translucent. Add mushrooms and cook until golden.
4. Lower heat, add chicken broth, and scrape any brown bits from the skillet. Stir in cream and Parmesan. Return chicken to the skillet.
5. Simmer for about 5 min until the sauce thickens. Toss in cooked pasta and coat well with the sauce.
6. Serve garnished with fresh parsley.

TIPS:

- Substitute with whole wheat pasta for a healthier option.
- Add a splash of white wine to the sauce for extra depth.

N.V.: Calories: 720, Fat: 32g, Carbs: 67g, Protein: 38g, Sugar: 4g

MUSHROOM AND CARAMELIZED ONION TART

PREPARATION TIME: 20 min - **COOKING TIME:** 40 min
MODE OF COOKING: Baking - **SERVINGS:** 6
INGREDIENTS:

- 1 pre-made pie crust
- 1 lb. mixed mushrooms (such as cremini, shiitake, and oyster), sliced
- 2 large onions, thinly sliced
- 1/4 cup sour cream
- 1/4 cup whole milk
- 2 eggs
- 2 Tbsp unsalted butter
- 2 Tbsp olive oil
- 1 tsp sugar
- 1 tsp thyme leaves
- Salt and pepper to taste
- 1/4 cup grated Gruyere cheese

DIRECTIONS:

1. Preheat oven to 375°F (190°C).
2. In a large skillet, heat butter and 1 Tbsp olive oil over medium heat. Add onions and sugar, cook, stirring occasionally until deeply caramelized, about 20-25 min.
3. In another skillet, heat the remaining olive oil. Add mushrooms and sauté until golden and tender, about 10 min.
4. In a bowl, whisk together sour cream, milk, eggs, thyme, salt, and pepper.
5. Spread caramelized onions on the bottom of the pie crust, followed by sautéed mushrooms. Pour the sour cream mixture over the top and sprinkle with Gruyere cheese.
6. Bake in the preheated oven for 30-35 min until the filling is set and the crust is golden brown.

TIPS:

- Let the tart cool for a few minutes before slicing to allow the filling to set properly.
- This tart pairs wonderfully with a light arugula salad dressed with a simple lemon vinaigrette.

N.V.: Calories: 350, Fat: 22g, Carbs: 28g, Protein: 9g, Sugar: 6g

These recipes are crafted to bring out the best in the mushrooms you've cultivated, celebrating their diversity and your hard work. Whether it's a hearty pasta or a delicate tart, mushrooms add depth and delight to every dish. Enjoy the process of cooking as much as the final taste, and let each meal be a reflection of your journey in mushroom cultivation.

GRILLED MUSHROOMS WITH HERB BUTTER

PREPARATION TIME: 10 min - **COOKING TIME:** 10 min
MODE OF COOKING: Grilling - **SERVINGS:** 4
INGREDIENTS:

- 1 lb. large mushrooms (such as Portobello, shiitake, or oyster), cleaned and stems removed
- 4 Tbsp unsalted butter, softened
- 1 Tbsp fresh parsley, finely chopped
- 1 tsp fresh rosemary, finely chopped
- 1 clove garlic, minced
- Salt and freshly ground black pepper
- Lemon wedges, for serving

DIRECTIONS:
1. Preheat grill to medium-high heat (about 375°F / 190°C).
2. In a small bowl, mix together butter, parsley, rosemary, garlic, salt, and pepper until well combined.
3. Brush the mushrooms with the herb butter, ensuring both sides are well coated.

4. Place mushrooms on the grill, cooking for about 5 min per side, or until they are tender and have grill marks.

5. Serve hot with additional herb butter dolloped on top and a squeeze of fresh lemon juice.

TIPS:

- For a smoky flavor, sprinkle a little smoked paprika into the butter mixture.
- Keep an eye on the mushrooms as they grill to prevent them from burning due to the butter.

N.V.: Calories: 150, Fat: 12g, Carbs: 6g, Protein: 3g, Sugar: 2g

These recipes are crafted to bring out the best in the mushrooms you've cultivated, celebrating their diversity and your hard work. Whether it's a hearty pasta or a delicate tart, mushrooms add depth and delight to every dish. Enjoy the process of cooking as much as the final taste, and let each meal be a reflection of your journey in mushroom cultivation.

MUSHROOM POLENTA BITES

PREPARATION TIME: 15 min - **COOKING TIME:** 30 min
MODE OF COOKING: Baking and Sautéing - **SERVINGS:** 6
INGREDIENTS:

- 1 cup polenta
- 3 cups water
- 1 tsp salt
- 2 Tbsp olive oil
- 1 lb. mixed mushrooms, finely chopped
- 2 cloves garlic, minced
- 1/4 cup grated Parmesan cheese
- Fresh thyme leaves for garnish

DIRECTIONS:

1. Bring water to a boil in a medium saucepan. Add salt and gradually whisk in polenta. Reduce heat and simmer, stirring frequently, until polenta is thick and creamy, about 20 min.

2. Spread cooked polenta onto a greased baking sheet, forming a thin layer. Allow to cool and set.

3. Preheat oven to 375°F (190°C).

4. In a skillet, heat olive oil over medium heat. Add garlic and mushrooms, sautéing until mushrooms are golden and tender.

5. Cut polenta into small squares and top each with a spoonful of mushroom mixture. Sprinkle with Parmesan cheese.

6. Bake in the preheated oven for 10 min until the cheese is melted and slightly golden.

7. Garnish with fresh thyme before serving.

TIPS:

- Serve these bites as an appetizer at your next party or as a savory snack.

N.V.: Calories: 180, Fat: 7g, Carbs: 23g, Protein: 6g, Sugar: 1g

ASIAN MUSHROOM STIR-FRY

PREPARATION TIME: 10 min - **COOKING TIME:** 15 min

MODE OF COOKING: Stir-Frying - **SERVINGS:** 4

INGREDIENTS:

- 1 lb. shiitake mushrooms, sliced
- 1 bell pepper, julienned
- 1 carrot, julienned
- 1 onion, sliced
- 2 Tbsp soy sauce
- 1 Tbsp sesame oil
- 1 tsp grated ginger
- 2 cloves garlic, minced
- 1 Tbsp hoisin sauce
- 2 tsp cornstarch dissolved in 2 Tbsp water
- 2 Tbsp vegetable oil

DIRECTIONS:

1. Heat vegetable oil in a large skillet or wok over high heat.

2. Add onion, garlic, and ginger, and sauté for 2 min until fragrant.

3. Add mushrooms, bell pepper, and carrot, and stir-fry for about 5-7 min until vegetables are tender but still crisp.

4. Stir in soy sauce, sesame oil, and hoisin sauce. Add the cornstarch mixture and stir well until the sauce thickens and becomes glossy.

5. Serve hot over steamed rice or noodles.

TIPS:

- Adjust the spiciness by adding chili flakes or a splash of chili sauce.

N.V.: Calories: 150, Fat: 8g, Carbs: 18g, Protein: 4g, Sugar: 5g

MUSHROOM AND WALNUT PÂTÉ

PREPARATION TIME: 10 min - **COOKING TIME:** 10 min

MODE OF COOKING: Blending - **SERVINGS:** 8

INGREDIENTS:

- 1 lb. button mushrooms, cleaned and chopped
- 1 cup walnuts, toasted
- 1 onion, chopped
- 2 cloves garlic, minced
- 2 Tbsp olive oil
- 2 Tbsp fresh parsley, chopped
- 1 Tbsp balsamic vinegar
- Salt and pepper to taste

DIRECTIONS:

1. In a skillet, heat olive oil over medium heat. Add onion and garlic and sauté until onion is translucent.

2. Add mushrooms and cook until they are soft and all their moisture has evaporated.

3. Transfer mushroom mixture to a food processor, add walnuts, parsley, and balsamic vinegar. Blend until smooth.

4. Season with salt and pepper. Chill in the refrigerator for at least an hour before serving.

TIPS:

- Serve chilled with crusty bread or crackers for a delightful appetizer.

N.V.: Calories: 190, Fat: 15g, Carbs: 10g, Protein: 5g, Sugar: 2g

MUSHROOM AND HERB OMELETTE

PREPARATION TIME: 5 min - **COOKING TIME:** 10 min

MODE OF COOKING: Frying - **SERVINGS:** 2

INGREDIENTS:

- 4 eggs
  - 1/2 lb. fresh mixed mushrooms, sliced
  - 1 Tbsp fresh chives, chopped
  - 1 Tbsp fresh parsley, chopped
  - 2 Tbsp unsalted butter
  - Salt and pepper to taste

DIRECTIONS:

1. In a mixing bowl, beat eggs with salt, pepper, chives, and parsley.
2. In a non-stick skillet, melt butter over medium heat. Sauté mushrooms until golden and tender.
3. Pour egg mixture over mushrooms, cook over low heat until eggs are set but still slightly runny on top.
4. Fold the omelette in half and slide onto a plate. Serve immediately.

TIPS:

- Add grated cheese for extra richness.

N.V.: Calories: 300, Fat: 22g, Carbs: 6g, Protein: 18g, Sugar: 3g

BAKED MUSHROOM AND SPINACH FLATBREAD

PREPARATION TIME: 15 min - **COOKING TIME:** 15 min

MODE OF COOKING: Baking - **SERVINGS:** 4

INGREDIENTS:

- 1 pre-made flatbread or pizza base
- 1/2 lb. fresh spinach, washed and roughly chopped
- 1/2 lb. mixed mushrooms, sliced
- 1 garlic clove, minced
- 1/4 cup ricotta cheese

- 1/2 cup mozzarella cheese, shredded
- 2 Tbsp olive oil
- Salt and pepper to taste

DIRECTIONS:

1. Preheat oven to 400°F (204°C).
2. In a skillet, heat 1 Tbsp olive oil over medium heat. Add garlic and mushrooms, sauté until mushrooms are tender.
3. Add spinach to the skillet, cook until just wilted. Remove from heat.
4. Spread ricotta cheese over the flatbread, then top with the mushroom and spinach mixture. Sprinkle mozzarella cheese on top.
5. Drizzle with remaining olive oil and season with salt and pepper.
6. Bake in the preheated oven for about 15 min until the edges are crisp and the cheese is bubbly and golden.

TIPS:

- For a crispy base, pre-bake the flatbread for 5 min before adding toppings.

N.V.: Calories: 280, Fat: 18g, Carbs: 21g, Protein: 12g, Sugar: 2g

These recipes provide a diverse range of options for incorporating mushrooms into your meals, from simple appetizers to hearty main courses. Enjoy exploring these flavors and textures as you make the most of your mushroom harvest.

PRESERVING YOUR MUSHROOMS: DRYING, CANNING, AND MORE

The joy of harvesting mushrooms doesn't have to end with the current season. Preserving these earthy treasures extends the delight of your hard work into the months and even years ahead. Whether through drying, canning, or other

innovative methods, each technique has its charm and purpose, keeping the essence of your harvest alive and well for future culinary creations.

The Art of Drying Mushrooms

Drying is perhaps the oldest and most straightforward method of preserving mushrooms. The process is simple: by removing moisture, you inhibit the growth of microorganisms and enzymes that would otherwise cause decay. What remains are dried specimens that can retain their flavor and nutritional value for years when stored properly.

Steps for Drying Mushrooms:

1. **Clean and Prepare:** Begin by gently brushing your mushrooms clean. It's crucial to avoid washing them, if possible, as extra moisture can extend the drying time. Slice the mushrooms uniformly to ensure even drying.

2. **Choosing a Drying Method:** You can dry mushrooms in several ways:
   - **Air Drying:** Ideal for less humid climates; string the mushrooms and hang them in a dry, ventilated area.
   - **Oven Drying:** Set your oven at a low temperature, around 150°F (65°C). Place mushroom slices on a baking sheet in a single layer, and leave the oven door slightly open to allow moisture to escape. Check and flip the mushrooms every hour until completely dry.
   - **Dehydrator:** If you have a dehydrator, follow the manufacturer's instructions. Typically, you'll set the temperature between 125°F and 135°F (52°C - 57°C) and dry them for 4 to 6 hours.

3. **Storage:** Once dried, store the mushrooms in an airtight container in a cool, dark place. They can last for several years but are best used within a year for optimum flavor.

Uses for Dried Mushrooms: Rehydrate them in warm water or stock for 20 to 30 minutes and use them in soups, stews, and sauces. The liquid used for rehydration is imbued with a deep mushroom flavor and makes an excellent base for dishes.

Canning Mushrooms

Canning is another reliable preservation method, especially for those who enjoy mushrooms as part of their pantry staples. It involves sterilizing and sealing them in airtight containers, usually glass jars, to prevent spoilage.

Steps for Canning Mushrooms:

1. **Preparation:** Clean the mushrooms and cut them into uniform sizes to ensure even processing. Blanch in boiling water for 5 minutes to halt enzyme activity.

2. **Packing the Jars:** Place the blanched mushrooms in sterilized canning jars. You can add a pinch of salt or some herbs like thyme or rosemary for extra flavor.

3. **Covering with Liquid:** Fill the jars with a hot pickling solution (usually a mix of vinegar, water, and spices) or a simple brine to cover the mushrooms, leaving about half an inch of headspace.

4. **Sealing and Processing:** Seal the jars with lids and rings, then process them in a boiling water bath or a pressure canner according to the altitude and your canner's instructions. This step is crucial as it kills any remaining microorganisms and seals the jars hermetically.

5. **Storage:** Store the canned mushrooms in a cool, dark place. They can typically last for up to a year. Once opened, keep refrigerated and use within a week.

Uses for Canned Mushrooms: They are excellent in pasta dishes, casseroles, or as a ready-to-use addition to quick meals.

Freezing Mushrooms

Freezing is perhaps the easiest method of preserving mushrooms and one that maintains their texture and flavor quite well.

Steps for Freezing Mushrooms:

1. **Preparation:** Clean the mushrooms and slice them if they are large. Smaller mushrooms can be frozen whole.

2. **Blanching:** To preserve their color and flavor, blanch the mushrooms first. Boil them for a couple of minutes, then plunge into ice water to stop the cooking process.

3. **Drying and Packing:** Pat the mushrooms dry. Spread them on a baking sheet in a single layer and freeze them until solid. Once frozen, transfer the mushrooms to airtight bags or containers.

4. **Storage:** Keep them frozen until ready to use. They can be stored for up to a year.

Uses for Frozen Mushrooms: Use them directly from the freezer in cooked dishes such as stir-fries, soups, and stews.

Other Preservation Methods

Pickling: An excellent way to preserve the unique flavors of mushrooms, pickling involves immersing them in a solution of vinegar, water, salt, and spices. The acidic environment prevents bacterial growth, extending the shelf life of your mushrooms while infusing them with flavor.

Making Mushroom Powder: Mushroom powder is made by grinding dried mushrooms into a fine dust. It can be used as a flavor enhancer in recipes, adding a rich umami kick to dishes ranging from scrambled eggs to soups.

Preserving mushrooms allows you to capture the essence of your harvest in a multitude of forms, each with its unique advantages. Whether dried, canned, frozen, pickled, or transformed into powder, these methods ensure that you can enjoy the fruits of your mushroom cultivation well beyond their typical fresh lifespan, bringing the taste of the forest and field to your table throughout the year.

CHAPTER 12: MYCOLOGICAL COMMUNITIES AND FURTHER LEARNING

Mushroom cultivation is more than just a solitary pursuit; it thrives on community and collective wisdom. In this chapter, we delve into the vibrant world of mycological communities and the avenues for further learning that can enrich your understanding and enhance your practice. As mushroom growers, we share a unique bond—an intrinsic connection to the earth and its most secretive yet generous organisms. Here, we explore how joining forces with fellow enthusiasts can transform a personal hobby into a shared passion, fostering not only individual growth but also contributing to a larger environmental consciousness.

The journey of a mushroom cultivator is continuous, filled with constant learning and delightful discoveries. Whether you're a novice seeking guidance or an experienced grower looking to exchange advanced techniques, the mycological community offers a treasure trove of resources. From local mushroom clubs to global online forums, these networks serve as hubs of knowledge and support where ideas and spores alike can spread with equal fervor.

This chapter is not just a guide to joining or building networks but an invitation to participate in a dialogue that spans generations and continents. It's here, in the exchange of stories and strategies, that many cultivators find their most rewarding experiences. By engaging with these communities, you gain access to a collective knowledge base that is both vast and nuanced, encompassing traditional practices and cutting-edge innovations.

As you turn these pages, consider how you might not only grow mushrooms but also grow within and contribute to this thriving community. Here's to expanding your horizons, deepening your connections, and enriching your practice through the shared joy of mushroom cultivation. Let's explore how these communal experiences can illuminate new paths on your mycological journey, leading to richer harvests— not just of mushrooms, but of knowledge and friendships too.

JOINING MUSHROOM CLUBS AND ONLINE COMMUNITIES

Mushroom cultivation, while often a solitary endeavor, blossoms in a community setting where ideas, experiences, and spores are exchanged freely among enthusiasts. Joining a mushroom club or engaging with an online community can significantly enrich your cultivation experience. These groups provide not only practical advice and support but also a sense of camaraderie among those who share a passion for fungi.

The Benefits of Joining Mushroom Clubs

Mushroom clubs are typically local or regional organizations that gather enthusiasts from all walks of life, from professional mycologists to hobbyist growers. These clubs often organize regular meetings, field trips, and foraging excursions, which are invaluable for learning about local mushroom species, foraging safety, and sustainable harvesting practices.

Networking and Knowledge Exchange: One of the primary benefits of joining a mushroom club is the direct line to a community's cumulative knowledge. More experienced members can offer insights into advanced cultivation techniques or help identify and resolve issues you might encounter in your growing endeavors.

Educational Workshops and Speakers: Many clubs invite experts to speak on various topics related to mycology, such as fungal biology, cultivation methods, and the environmental impacts of mushrooms. These sessions can provide deeper scientific insights and practical advice that are not readily available in books or online.

Community Projects: Some clubs engage in community projects like restoring natural habitats, organizing mushroom shows, or even collaborating with local schools to educate children about the importance of fungi in ecosystems. Participating in these projects can be incredibly fulfilling as it allows you to contribute to conservation efforts and spread awareness about the ecological importance of mushrooms.

Thriving in Online Mycological Communities

In today's digital age, online communities have become just as pivotal as local clubs. Websites, forums, and social media platforms like Facebook, Reddit, and Instagram offer global networks where mushroom enthusiasts can connect, share, and learn from each other.

Accessibility and Diversity: Online forums are accessible around the clock, allowing you to post questions and receive answers from across the globe. This accessibility can be especially beneficial if you live in a region where local mycological societies are non-existent or inactive.

Photo Sharing and Identification Help: Many online communities offer platforms where members can share photos of their finds and receive help with identification from experienced foragers and mycologists. This practice is not only helpful for ensuring safety and accuracy in identification but also serves as a valuable learning tool.

Special Interest Groups: Whatever your specific interest in the field of mycology—be it the scientific study of fungi, culinary applications, medicinal uses, or artistic endeavors with mushroom dyes—there is likely an online group dedicated to that niche. These specialized forums can provide resources and connections that are tailored to your particular interests.

Getting the Most Out of Mushroom Clubs and Online Communities

Active Participation: Like any community, you get out what you put in. Active participation by attending meetings, joining outings, and contributing to discussions online can enhance your learning and establish stronger connections within the community.

Volunteering: Many clubs and online groups thrive on volunteer effort. Offering to help with organizing events, managing websites, or leading projects not only contributes to the group but can also enhance your leadership skills and deepen your engagement with the community.

Continual Learning: The field of mycology is ever-evolving with new research, techniques, and discoveries. Staying engaged with a community keeps you updated on the latest developments and innovations in mushroom cultivation and mycology at large.

Potential Challenges and Considerations

Regional Differences: Not all advice may be applicable universally, especially when it comes to foraging and cultivating in different climates and ecosystems. Always consider local conditions and regulations when applying advice from global or even national online platforms.

Quality of Information: While there is a wealth of information available, the accuracy can vary. It's important to verify critical information, especially regarding mushroom identification and consumption, through reputable sources or confirmation from multiple experienced individuals.

Balancing Online and In-Person Engagements: While online communities offer great flexibility and accessibility, they can sometimes lack the personal touch and hands-on learning experiences that local clubs provide. Balancing both online and in-person interactions can lead to a more holistic experience.

In sum, mushroom clubs and online communities offer a rich tapestry of learning opportunities, support, and camaraderie for mushroom enthusiasts. By joining these groups, you not only enhance your own cultivation skills and knowledge but also contribute to a broader community of like-minded individuals who share a passion for these remarkable organisms. Whether through local clubs or global online networks, the connections you make and the knowledge you gain can profoundly enrich your mushroom cultivation journey and help foster a greater appreciation for the fungal kingdom

RECOMMENDED BOOKS, JOURNALS, AND WEBSITES

As you deepen your journey into the world of mycology, surrounding yourself with a rich array of resources can illuminate your path. Books, journals, and websites not only offer a foundation of knowledge but also keep you updated on the latest research, trends, and community insights. Here, we explore a selection of key resources that every mushroom enthusiast—beginner or expert—should consider.

Essential Books on Mushroom Cultivation and Mycology

"Mycelium Running: How Mushrooms Can Help Save the World" by Paul Stamets

This book is a groundbreaking resource for anyone interested in environmental sustainability and mycology. Stamets explores the role of mushrooms in ecological restoration and their potential to revolutionize environmental cleanup strategies.

"The Mushroom Cultivator: A Practical Guide to Growing Mushrooms at Home" by Paul Stamets and J.S. Chilton

Perfect for beginners and advanced cultivators alike, this comprehensive guide details various methods of mushroom cultivation, with practical advice on substrates, pest management, and the biology of fungi.

"Entangled Life: How Fungi Make Our Worlds, Change Our Minds & Shape Our Futures" by Merlin Sheldrake

In this compelling read, Sheldrake delves into the fascinating biological roles of fungi. This book provides a broader understanding of how essential fungi are to life on Earth, beyond their use in cultivation.

"Mushrooms of the World with Pictures to Color" by Jeannette Bowers

This unique book combines information with engagement, offering coloring pages of mushrooms alongside descriptive text. It's a wonderful resource for visual learners and those interested in the artistic aspects of mycology.

Influential Journals and Periodicals

Mycology

This peer-reviewed journal is dedicated to the study of fungi, including their molecular genetics, biology, and pathology. It's an invaluable resource for those looking to deepen their scientific understanding of mycology.

Fungal Diversity

An international journal that publishes comprehensive papers on all aspects of fungal biology. It explores the biodiversity, ecological roles, and biotechnological applications of fungi.

The Mycophile

Published by the North American Mycological Association, this newsletter offers articles on mushroom identification, book reviews, and news from the mycological community.

Websites for Continuous Learning and Connection

MushroomExpert.Com

A comprehensive online resource that provides detailed descriptions, photographs, and keys for identifying mushrooms. It is particularly useful for both novice foragers and experienced mycologists.

Fungi Perfect

Founded by Paul Stamets, this website not only sells mushroom cultivation supplies but also offers a wealth of information on mushroom cultivation techniques and mycological research.

The Shroyer

This online community is one of the most extensive forums for discussing all things mushrooms. It includes detailed guides on cultivation, identification forums, and a vibrant community ready to answer questions and share experiences.

Mycological Society Websites

Many local and national mycological societies maintain websites filled with resources for local foragers and cultivators. These often include event listings, educational materials, and forums for member interaction.

Leveraging These Resources

Integrating Knowledge: While books provide a solid foundation, journals and websites offer ongoing updates and community interaction, which are crucial for staying current in the rapidly evolving field of mycology.

Expanding Your Network: Utilizing these resources often leads to opportunities for networking. Many books and websites encourage participation in community science projects or local mycological societies.

Practical Application: Apply what you learn by experimenting with different cultivation techniques or participating in local foraging and identification activities. The practical application of knowledge not only solidifies learning but also enhances your overall experience and success as a cultivator.

The Importance of Credible Sources

In a field as specific and scientifically rich as mycology, ensuring the credibility of your resources is paramount. Opt for books that are well-reviewed by experts in the field, and prioritize journals that are peer-reviewed. Websites should be evaluated for their authority, accuracy, and up-to-date content to ensure that you are receiving reliable information.

In conclusion, enriching your library with these suggested books, journals, and websites will empower you to grow in expertise and confidence. Whether your interest lies in the practical aspects of mushroom cultivation, the scientific study of fungi, or the ecological impacts of mycology, there are resources available to support every facet of your learning journey. Dive into these materials with a curious mind, and allow them to guide you towards becoming not just a skilled cultivator, but a knowledgeable and passionate mycologist.

CHAPTER 13: THE FUTURE OF MUSHROOM CULTIVATION

As we near the close of our comprehensive journey through the art and science of mushroom cultivation, it's essential to gaze into the horizon and ponder what the future might hold for this fascinating field. The advancements in mycology and its application in sustainable agriculture present us with a tapestry of possibilities, promising significant shifts not only in how we cultivate but also in how we view the role of fungi in our world.

In recent years, the surge in interest towards fungi has not been solely among those who cherish the forest floor or the culinary adventurers but has increasingly included technologists, environmentalists, and innovators. These diverse perspectives are converging to push the boundaries of traditional mycology into realms previously imagined only in the pages of science fiction.

Consider the role of biotechnology in mushroom cultivation: genetically edited mushrooms that resist pests more effectively, or mycelium that can be engineered to break down plastic waste. These innovations are not just on drawing boards but are beginning to take shape in laboratories and small-scale test fields. This technological infusion does not strip away the natural essence of mycology but enhances our ability to harness these organisms for the greater good.

Beyond the lab, the landscape of mushroom cultivation is also being transformed by a growing community of growers who are integrating sophisticated data analytics to optimize yield and sustainability. Imagine a future where every mushroom cultivator has access to cloud-based AI systems that provide insights into the precise conditions needed for various species, from moisture levels to nutrient ratios. This digital revolution in cultivation is democratizing the ability to grow mushrooms efficiently, making it accessible to more people around the globe.

As we look forward, it is not just about the technological enhancements but also about the cultural shift towards more sustainable and responsible food production systems. Mushrooms are at the heart of this shift, offering solutions to food security, environmental sustainability, and even urban agricultural practices. The future of mushroom cultivation is bright, filled with innovations that will continue to surprise us, challenge us, and inspire us to think differently about the humble fungi that have so much to offer.

TECHNOLOGICAL ADVANCES

In the realm of mushroom cultivation, the integration of technology not only reshapes our current practices but also seeds the ground for future innovations that could revolutionize the industry. As we delve into the technological advances shaping this future, it becomes clear that the field of mycology is experiencing a renaissance, spurred by breakthroughs that bridge biology with cutting-edge technology.

The Digital Transformation of Mycology

One of the most significant shifts in mushroom cultivation is the adoption of digital tools that enhance precision and efficiency. Innovators in the sector are leveraging technologies like the Internet of Things (IoT) to create interconnected systems where environmental conditions are continuously monitored and adjusted in real time. Sensors placed in mushroom growing environments can track temperature, humidity, CO_2 levels, and light intensity, providing a torrent of data that, when analyzed, offers insights far beyond what the unaided eye can discern.

This data-driven approach allows for the automation of climate control in growing facilities, ensuring optimal conditions for mushroom growth. Automated systems can adjust parameters instantly in response to data from sensors, reducing the likelihood of human error and the labor traditionally involved in monitoring crops. This not only boosts productivity but also improves the consistency and quality of the yield.

Artificial Intelligence and Machine Learning

Further on the technological horizon, Artificial Intelligence (AI) and Machine Learning (ML) are beginning to play pivotal roles. These technologies are not just analytical tools but also predictive ones. AI algorithms can predict yield rates based on patterns observed over time, advising cultivators on the best times to scale up or down their production. More advanced AI models are being trained to recognize signs of disease or pest infestation, alerting growers to potential issues before they become visible.

Machine learning models, trained on vast datasets, can optimize growing conditions for new strains of mushrooms, speeding up the experimentation process that once took years. This rapid testing and adaptation enhance our ability to develop mushroom varieties with specific traits, such as increased nutritional content or enhanced medicinal qualities.

Robotics in Mushroom Farms

Robotics also finds its place in the modern mushroom farm, handling tasks ranging from the mixing of substrates to the delicate process of harvesting. Robotics technology can be particularly transformative in the harvesting phase, where precision and delicacy are paramount. Robots equipped with vision systems can identify when mushrooms are at the perfect stage of growth for picking, ensuring that they are harvested at their peak. This not only maximizes the quality and extends the shelf life of mushrooms but also reduces waste significantly.

Moreover, robotics helps address one of the biggest challenges in agriculture: labor shortages. With robots taking on repetitive and labor-intensive tasks, human workers can be redeployed to more skilled positions, such as system management and optimization, further improving operational efficiency.

Blockchain for Traceability

On the consumer side, traceability and transparency in food production have become increasingly important. Here, blockchain technology offers a promising solution. By recording data on a blockchain at every step of the supply chain—from spore to store—consumers can trace the journey of their food. This technology ensures that data is immutable and transparent, increasing consumer trust. For mushroom cultivators, blockchain not only supports marketing and sales but also enhances logistical efficiency, allowing for better management of the supply chain.

Biotechnological Enhancements

Beyond digital technology, biotechnological advancements are enabling us to manipulate the very building blocks of fungal organisms. Genetic engineering and CRISPR technology open up possibilities for developing mushroom strains that are more resilient to climate changes, have higher yields, or possess specific flavor profiles. This genetic tweaking does raise ethical and regulatory questions, but it also holds the potential to create mushroom varieties that can thrive in diverse climates, making mushroom cultivation more accessible worldwide.

The Integration of Mycology with Other Biotechnologies

Mycology is not standing alone in its technological evolution. It is being integrated with other biotechnologies to create novel solutions to global issues. For instance, mycelium-based materials are being developed as sustainable alternatives to plastics and building materials. These materials are not only biodegradable but also have the potential to be 'grown' under controlled conditions, reducing reliance on traditional manufacturing and its associated environmental impacts.

Mushrooms are also being explored as bio-remediators in polluted environments. Their natural ability to break down complex compounds can be enhanced through biotechnological means, enabling them to clean soils contaminated with heavy metals or pesticides more effectively.

Conclusion

As we look to the future, the intersection of technology and mushroom cultivation holds limitless potential. These advancements are not merely about enhancing production; they are about transforming the role of fungi in our ecosystems and economies. They promise a future where mushroom cultivation is not only a source of nutrition and healing but also a cornerstone of sustainable practices globally.

In embracing these technologies, we must proceed with caution, ensuring that our innovations align with ethical standards and contribute positively to our environment. Yet, with thoughtful integration of technology, the future of mushroom cultivation looks not only promising but also exciting, as it moves us closer to a sustainable and food-secure world.

THE ROLE OF MUSHROOMS IN SUSTAINABILITY

Mushrooms, those enigmatic entities of the forest floor, are stepping into the light as powerful allies in our quest for sustainability. Their unique biological characteristics and their roles within ecosystems highlight their potential not just as a food source, but as crucial components in the sustainable practices that are becoming essential to modern agriculture, urban planning, and environmental management.

Mushrooms are a cornerstone in the architecture of nature's recycling system. They break down organic materials, returning nutrients to the soil while detoxifying some environmental contaminants. This natural capacity for decomposition and remediation is being leveraged in new and innovative ways to address human-created problems, ranging from waste management to pollution reduction.

Bioremediation: Cleaning Up Our Act

One of the most promising roles for mushrooms in sustainability is in bioremediation—the process of using living organisms to remove or neutralize contaminants from a polluted area. Fungi are particularly adept at this task because of their mycelial network, which can spread through soil and absorb or neutralize pollutants like pesticides, heavy metals, and even oil spills. Experiments with fungi such as oyster mushrooms have shown that they can not only thrive on petroleum-based contaminants but actually break them down into harmless substances.

This application is increasingly important as we grapple with the legacies of industrial pollution. Mushroom-based bioremediation offers a natural, less invasive solution compared to traditional methods, which often involve removing large quantities of soil or adding chemical treatments that can cause further harm.

Urban Mushroom Farms: Local Solutions

As urban populations continue to grow, the concept of local food production becomes more crucial. Urban mushroom farming is emerging as a viable solution due to mushrooms' minimal space requirements and their ability to grow on various organic waste products. These urban farms can help reduce food miles, the distance food travels from production to consumer, which contributes to lower greenhouse gas emissions.

Moreover, urban mushroom cultivation transforms waste management strategies by turning organic waste into a valuable commodity. Coffee grounds, paper waste, and wood chips can all be substrates for growing edible mushrooms. This not only helps reduce the volume of waste destined for landfills but also provides local communities with fresh, nutritious food.

Climate Change Mitigation: A Fungal Fix?

Mushrooms might also play a direct role in combating climate change. Through the process of carbon sequestration, fungi can help lock carbon away in soils. Mycelium acts as a natural binder, aggregating soil particles and storing carbon within their structures. This storage capability is critical as increasing soil carbon content can significantly mitigate the atmospheric CO_2 levels that contribute to climate change. Furthermore, the development of mycelium-based materials as alternatives to plastics offers another avenue through which mushrooms can impact sustainability.

These materials are not only biodegradable but can be produced with significantly lower energy compared to conventional plastics, reducing the carbon footprint of the materials we use daily.

Sustainable Agricultural Practices: Mycorrhizal Magic

Mushrooms also contribute to sustainable agriculture through their symbiotic relationships with plants. Mycorrhizal fungi, which form associations with plant roots, enhance plant health and soil quality. They improve plant nutrient uptake, which can decrease the need for chemical fertilizers, reducing runoff and soil degradation. The enhanced nutrient uptake also leads to healthier, more resilient plants, reducing the need for chemical pesticides and further contributing to an agricultural approach that is more in harmony with nature.

The Circular Economy: Mushrooms as a Keystone

In a broader sense, mushrooms epitomize the principles of a circular economy—a system aimed at eliminating waste and the continual use of resources. Mushroom cultivation can be integrated into agricultural and industrial systems to create closed-loop cycles where waste from one process becomes the input for another. For example, spent mushroom substrate, rich in nutrients after the cultivation cycle, can be used as a soil amendment, returning organic material and nutrients back to the earth.

Educating and Engaging Communities

Finally, the role of mushrooms in sustainability extends beyond environmental impacts to include social dimensions. Community-based mushroom projects can educate the public about ecological stewardship, fostering a deeper connection with the environment and promoting sustainable practices across different sectors of society.

These projects can serve as powerful educational tools, demonstrating the principles of ecology, biology, and sustainability in tangible, interactive ways. They empower communities, particularly in urban areas, by providing the skills and knowledge to grow food locally and sustainably, promoting food security and resilience against food system shocks.

Looking Ahead

As we look towards the future, the role of mushrooms in sustainability is only expected to grow. Their ability to address environmental, social, and economic challenges simultaneously positions them as a crucial component of sustainable practices. Whether through cleaning contaminated lands, reducing waste, providing nutritious food, or educating the public, mushrooms have much to offer in our pursuit of a more sustainable planet.

By embracing these roles and integrating mushrooms into our sustainability strategies, we not only leverage their ecological benefits but also inspire a shift in how we interact with and perceive our natural world. The future of sustainability may indeed have a fungal heart, pulsing quietly but powerfully beneath the surface, ready to emerge as a symbol of ecological resilience and regeneration.

APPENDICES

As we reach the appendices of this guide, we find ourselves at a treasure trove of supplemental resources designed to enhance and expand your mushroom cultivation journey. The appendices are akin to the toolshed in a gardener's plot— here, you'll find every specialized tool and resource to refine your craft, answer lingering questions, and perhaps solve those peculiar puzzles that the main chapters stirred in your curious mind.

This section is structured to provide quick, accessible reference materials that span a comprehensive list of mushroom varieties, a glossary of mycological terms, additional online resources, and a frequently asked questions compendium. Each of these resources is intended to complement the detailed discussions we've traversed so far, offering a handy back-pocket guide that you can return to time and again.

The glossary will demystify the scientific jargon, breaking down complex terms into digestible definitions that reinforce your understanding. Meanwhile, the comprehensive list of mushroom varieties celebrates the biodiversity of fungi, serving as a visual and descriptive catalog for both common and exotic species, enriching your choices for cultivation.

Moreover, the additional online resources are curated to guide you to further reading, connect you with online communities, and help you discover suppliers that align with the ethical and sustainable practices emphasized throughout this book. This network will support and expand your growing passion, connecting you with like-minded enthusiasts and experts.

Finally, the FAQs address those recurring questions that might have echoed through the chapters, providing clarifications and practical advice in a straightforward format. This section ensures that no reader, whether novice or seasoned grower, leaves with unanswered queries.

By providing these appendices, the goal is to equip you with a comprehensive toolkit that empowers your continued exploration and success in the artful science of mushroom cultivation. Whether you're flipping back to find a quick definition or seeking inspiration for your next cultivation project, these resources are designed to support your growth as a cultivator and enthusiast.

A: GLOSSARY OF MYCOLOGICAL TERMS

Navigating the language of mycology can be as intricate and fascinating as the study of mushrooms themselves. This glossary serves as your compass through the diverse terminology used in mushroom cultivation. It's designed not just for clarity, but also to deepen your understanding of the subject, helping you to engage more confidently with the broader community of mycologists and enthusiasts.

Mycelium

This is the vegetative part of a fungus, consisting of a network of fine white filaments (hyphae) that branch and spread underground or within decaying plant material. Mycelium is the main growth phase of the fungus, absorbing nutrients from the environment to sustain growth and eventually produce mushrooms, the reproductive structures.

Hyphae

The plural of hypha, these are the thread-like structures that make up the mycelium of a fungus. Each hypha is a tubular cell that grows at its tip, extending into new territories and absorbing nutrients through its wall.

Spore

Spores are microscopic reproductive units of fungi, equivalent to seeds in the plant kingdom. They are produced by the millions in the gills or pores of a mushroom and can travel by air or water to colonize new environments. Each spore has the potential to grow into a new mycelial network.

Substrate

The substrate is any material that provides nutrients and support for the growth of mushrooms. Common substrates in mushroom cultivation include straw, wood chips, sawdust, and compost. The choice of substrate often depends on the mushroom species being cultivated.

Inoculation

This process involves introducing mushroom spores or mycelium into a substrate to begin the cultivation process. Inoculation must be done under conditions that minimize contamination from other fungi or bacteria.

Fruiting Body

The fruiting body of a fungus is what most people recognize as a mushroom. It is the reproductive structure that grows from the mycelium when environmental conditions are favorable (such as the right temperature, humidity, and light).

Spawn

Spawn is mycelium that has been grown on a small amount of substrate to a stage where it's ready to colonize a larger amount of substrate. It is essentially the "seed" used to grow mushrooms in cultivation, often made from grains like rye or millet that have been fully colonized by mycelium.

Sterilization

Sterilization involves the complete elimination of all microbial life from a substrate or piece of equipment. This is typically achieved through methods such as autoclaving (using pressurized steam) or chemical sterilant. Sterilization is crucial in mushroom cultivation to prevent contamination by unwanted organisms.

Pasteurization

Unlike sterilization, pasteurization does not kill all microbes but reduces their number to a level where the mushroom mycelium can outcompete them. This is often done by heating the substrate to a temperature that kills harmful bacteria and fungi without destroying beneficial organisms.

Colonization

This refers to the process by which mycelium grows through and fully occupies a substrate. Successful colonization is indicated by a white, thread-like network covering the substrate, signifying that the mycelium is healthy and ready to produce fruiting bodies.

Flush

A flush is a wave of mushroom fruiting bodies that sprout from the substrate. Many species of mushrooms do not fruit continuously but in several flushes, with periods of rest in between.

Gills

Located on the underside of a mushroom's cap, gills are thin, paper-like structures that radiate outward from the stalk. Spores are produced and released from the surfaces of these gills.

Stipe

The stipe is the stalk or stem of a mushroom that supports the cap and connects it to the mycelium or substrate. Not all mushrooms have a stipe, but for those that do, it's a defining feature in identification.

Lamella

These are another term for gills, but can also refer to ridges found under the caps of certain mushroom species which serve the same purpose of dispersing spores.

Pileus

The pileus is the scientific term for the cap of the mushroom—the umbrella-like structure that expands from the stipe. The pileus houses the reproductive structures of the fungus, such as gills or pores.

Mycorrhizal

Mycorrhizal fungi form a symbiotic association with the roots of plants. These relationships are crucial for nutrient exchange between soil and plant roots, enhancing plant growth and soil health. Mycorrhizal fungi can be ectomycorrhizal, forming sheaths around root tips, or endomycorrhizal, penetrating the root cells.

Each term in this glossary not only defines a part of the mushroom or its growth process but also invites you to delve deeper into the lifecycle and ecological roles of fungi. Whether you are scanning these terms while troubleshooting in your grow room or casually reading to bolster your fungal lexicon, this glossary is here to guide your understanding and enhance your discussions within the mycological community.

B: COMPREHENSIVE LIST OF MUSHROOM VARIETIES

Mushrooms, in their wondrous variety, offer a palette of flavors, textures, and benefits that can transform any garden, kitchen, or medicinal cabinet. From the familiar button mushrooms sprinkled on your salad to the exotic, medicinal rishi that brews a healing tea, each variety holds unique secrets and stories. This comprehensive list ventures through a curated selection of mushroom species, exploring their characteristics, culinary uses, and cultivation tips. As you familiarize yourself with these diverse forms of fungi, consider how each might find a place in your personal cultivation journey.

Agaricus Bosporus (Common Button Mushroom) This is perhaps the most well-known mushroom, found in grocery stores worldwide. It varies in color from white to light brown and grows readily on composted manure. It's excellent for beginners due to its forgiving nature in various growing conditions.

Pleurotus ostreatus (Oyster Mushroom) Known for their delicate texture and

FOREST MUSHROOMS
VECTOR CONCEPT

CHANTERELLE
HONEY AGARIC
CHAMPIGNON
AMANITA
BOLETUS
BROWN CAP BOLETUS
ORANGE CAP BOLETUS
RUSSULE

mild, sweet flavor, oyster mushrooms are one of the easiest to cultivate at home. They thrive on a variety of substrates, including coffee grounds and straw. Their shelf-like, oyster-shaped caps come in shades of white, grey, or even pink.

Lentinula edodes (Shiitake Mushroom) Valued for their rich, smoky flavor, shiitakes are popular in both culinary and medicinal contexts. They grow on hardwood logs or sawdust blocks and are renowned for their health benefits, including immune system support.

Ganoderma lucidum (Rishi Mushroom) Often called the "mushroom of immortality" in traditional Chinese medicine, rishi mushrooms are sought for their potential to enhance health and longevity. They are tougher and woodier than many other mushrooms, making them more suitable for teas and extracts than for typical culinary uses.

Hericium Erinaceus (Lion's Mane Mushroom) Distinctive for its cascading, icicle-like spines, lion's mane is as visually striking as it is beneficial for the brain and nervous system. This mushroom is best grown on hardwood substrates and is celebrated for its lobster-like flavor when cooked.

Marchella esculenta (Morel Mushroom) Highly coveted by gourmet chefs, morels are known for their honeycomb appearance. They are more challenging to cultivate than other varieties, often requiring specific soil conditions and temperature changes to fruit.

Taramites versicolor (Turkey Tail Mushroom) This mushroom is primarily known for its therapeutic properties, including its potential to support the immune system. Turkey tail grows on dead logs and stumps, presenting a colorful, fan-shaped array of stripes that resemble a turkey's tail.

Cordyceps sinensis (Cordyceps Mushroom) Famous for their unique growth on caterpillars in the wild, cultivated cordyceps offer similar health benefits without the need for such exotic cultivation methods. They are used in supplements for energy and athletic performance.

Agaricus surfaces (Almond Mushroom) This mushroom is appreciated for its almond-like taste and potential anti-cancer properties. It grows in composted substrates similar to the button mushroom but offers a more complex flavor profile.

Amanita muscaria (Fly Agaric) While iconic in appearance with its bright red cap and white spots, this mushroom is not edible and is known for its psychoactive properties. It serves more as a warning of the importance of proper identification than as a cultivation target.

Boletus edulis (Porcini Mushroom) A favorite in Italian cuisine, porcini mushrooms have a rich, nutty flavor. They are mycorrhizal, meaning they grow in symbiosis with the roots of living trees, which makes them challenging to cultivate outside of their natural woodland settings.

Craterless cornucopia (Black Trumpet Mushroom) These mushrooms are cherished for their smoky, rich flavor and trumpet-like shape. Like morels, they can be difficult to cultivate but are a prized find for foragers.

Psilocybin cogenesis (Magic Mushroom) Known for their psychoactive compounds, psilocybin mushrooms are used in spiritual and therapeutic practices. They grow on various substrates rich in nutrients, such as grains, but their cultivation and possession are illegal in many countries.

Pleurotus eryngium (King Oyster Mushroom) This robust variety is known for its thick, meaty stem and minimal cap. King oysters have a savory umami flavor and a firm texture that holds up well to cooking. Culturally adaptable, they can grow on a variety of lignocellulosic wastes, making them a popular choice for home cultivators.

Calvatia gigantea (Giant Puffball) Giant puffballs can grow to impressive sizes, sometimes weighing several pounds. They have a smooth, white exterior and a marshmallow-like texture when young. They are best when harvested young and cooked fresh, offering a mild, earthy flavor that makes a great substitute for tofu.

Grifols frondose (Maitake or Hen of the Woods) Maitake mushrooms grow at the base of trees, particularly oaks, in the wild. They are revered not only for their rich, woodsy taste but also for their potential health benefits, including immune system support and blood sugar regulation. Maitake can be cultivated on supplemented sawdust and requires specific humidity and temperature conditions to thrive.

Cnidocyte nuda (Blewit Mushroom) Blewits are easily recognizable by their violet cap and gills, and they offer a hearty, nutty flavor. They grow on composted leaf litter and are more tolerant of cold weather, often appearing in late fall or early winter. This variety requires careful identification as it can be confused with inedible or toxic species.

Flam Mulina volutes (Enoki Mushroom) Enoki mushrooms, with their long, slender stems and tiny caps, are a staple in East Asian cuisine, known for their crisp texture and delicate flavor. They thrive in cooler temperatures and can be grown on hardwood substrates or in bottles with a liquid culture.

Coprinus comates (Shaggy Mane) Shaggy mane is distinctive for its rapidly dissolving cap, which liquefies into a black ink soon after it's picked. This process is natural and is one reason why they must be cooked soon after harvesting. They have a delicate flavor, ideal for soups and sauces.

Stropharia rugosoannulata (Wine Cap Mushroom) Wine cap mushrooms are excellent for outdoor mushroom beds as they grow well on wood chips and straw. They have a slightly earthy and nutty flavor, making them a great addition to any dish that calls for mushrooms.

Pholidota Namiko (Namiko Mushroom) Namiko mushrooms are known for their sticky, gelatinous coating, which is highly prized in Japanese cooking for the rich texture it adds to soups and broths. These mushrooms require a well-maintained environment to cultivate, growing best on hardwood substrates.

Usti Lago maydis (Corn Smut or Huitlacoche) While considered a pest in the cornfields, huitlacoche is a delicacy in Mexican cuisine, where it is harvested and consumed as a fungal corn kernel mutation. It offers a smoky, savory flavor that is completely unlike typical corn.

Lactivores sulphurous (Chicken of the Woods) This bright orange or yellow mushroom grows on dead or dying trees and is known for its chicken-like texture and taste, making it a popular meat substitute. It requires specific conditions to cultivate but is a rewarding find for foragers.

Auricularia auricula-Judea (Wood Ear Mushroom) This jelly-like fungus is common in Asian dishes, known for its crunchy texture and ability to absorb flavors. Wood ear mushrooms thrive on decaying wood and are especially easy to identify due to their ear-like shape. They're excellent in soups and stir-fries, known for their health benefits, including improving circulation and lowering cholesterol.

Lactarium delicious (Saffron Milk Cap) Prized in European kitchens for their nutty, slightly peppery flavor, these mushrooms exude a saffron-colored milk when cut. They are mycorrhizal, making them challenging to cultivate commercially, but they are a popular target for foragers in pine forests.

Hypnum responsum (Hedgehog Mushroom) Unlike other mushrooms, hedgehogs have spines rather than gills under their cap, which give them a distinctive appearance and texture. They offer a sweet, nutty flavor that is much loved in gourmet cooking. Hedgehogs are ectomycorrhizal and grow in a symbiotic relationship with trees, making them another forager's favorite.

Pleurotus pulmonarias (Phoenix Oyster) Closely related to the more common oyster mushroom, the Phoenix oyster distinguishes itself by preferring slightly warmer climates. It shares the sweet, mild flavor and velvety texture of its relatives, making it just as versatile in the kitchen. Its ability to grow on a variety of organic substrates makes it popular among home cultivators.

Agrotype aegeriid (Poplar Mushroom) Known for its firm texture and intense flavor, the poplar mushroom, or velvet cioppino, is often used in Italian cooking. It grows naturally on dead hardwood, particularly poplar and cottonwood, and is another favorite among both commercial growers and hobbyists for its ease of cultivation.

Rusul virescens (Green Cracking Rusul) With a distinctive cracked, green cap, this mushroom is not only visually striking but also offers a crisp texture and mild flavor, perfect for fresh salads. Rusul mushrooms are mycorrhizal and notoriously difficult to cultivate, making them a prized find in wooded areas.

Entolimod abortive (Aborted Entolimod) This unique mushroom is known for its irregular shapes due to the way it grows in conjunction with honey mushrooms. The result is a meaty texture that is excellent in hearty dishes. Like many other wild species, cultivating Aborted Entolimod has not been commercially achieved, adding to its allure and mystery among mushroom hunters.

Paxil's involutes (Brown Roll-Rim) This mushroom is common in temperate forests but is noteworthy because it should be avoided due to its toxicity. It serves as a reminder of the importance of accurate identification and respect for the diverse capabilities of fungi, including those that are not beneficial to humans.

Tremella mesenterica (Witch's Butter) Bright yellow and brain-like in appearance, this gelatinous fungus is not only a curious sight but also has a history of use in traditional medicine, particularly in China. It grows on dead wood and is studied for its potential in medical applications, despite its bland flavor.

Polydorus squamosas (Dryad's Saddle) These mushrooms grow on decaying wood and are recognized by their large, fan-shaped caps and distinctive scale pattern. They offer a meaty texture, ideal for use in soups and stews, and are easiest to enjoy when harvested young and tender.

Spar Assis crisp (Cauliflower Mushroom) Resembling a sea coral or a ruffled cauliflower, this mushroom grows at the base of conifer trees. It's cherished for its crisp texture and sweet, nutty flavor, making it a fantastic addition to stir-fries and soups. The Cauliflower mushroom is also known for its antioxidant properties, adding to its allure as a functional food.

Cornellius micaceous (Mica Cap) These small, glistening mushrooms often appear in clusters on rotting wood. They are named for the mica-like particles on their caps. Mica caps are best eaten young before they start to auto-digest and turn into ink, a characteristic trait of the corrinoid mushrooms. They offer a mild flavor, suitable for quick sautés.

Chlorophyllin molybdites (False Parasol) Notorious for being one of the most common causes of mushroom poisoning, the False Parasol is crucial for foragers to recognize and avoid. It resembles the edible Parasol mushroom but can be distinguished by its green spores and unpleasant scent. This species is a reminder of the importance of careful identification in the gathering and consumption of wild mushrooms.

Sills luteus (Slippery Jack) Part of the bolete family, Slippery Jacks are known for their slimy, sticky caps and their preference for pine forests, where they form symbiotic mycorrhizal relationships with trees. While not the most celebrated culinary mushroom due to their texture, they can be delicious when properly prepared, particularly when dried or sautéed.

Ram aria Formosa (Beautiful Calvaria) This striking coral-like mushroom is another species that must be treated with caution due to its potential toxicity. Though it boasts a vibrant, branched appearance that can be quite beautiful, consuming it can result in gastrointestinal distress, highlighting the need for precise identification.

Glucinum scab rum (Birch Bolete) Found under birch trees with which they form symbiotic relationships, Birch Boletes have a robust, earthy flavor that makes them favored by mushroom enthusiasts. They are particularly good in dishes that allow their strong flavor to shine, such as stews and roasts.

Macrolepiota proceri (Parasol Mushroom) The Parasol Mushroom is highly prized for its large size and distinctive appearance, with a tall, slender stalk and a large, umbrella-like cap. It has a meaty texture and a delicate flavor, ideal for frying. This mushroom is a forager's favorite and offers a satisfying find in grassy meadows.

Hericium Americanum (Bear's Head Tooth) A close relative to Lion's Mane, the Bear's Head Tooth mushroom is sought after for its tender, meaty texture and its resemblance to seafood in both taste and texture. Like its cousin, it is also known for its potential benefits in supporting nerve growth and overall brain health.

Gea strum saccate (Earthstar) This mushroom is more often admired for its unique appearance than eaten. Its star-like segments peel back to reveal a central spore sac. Earthstars are a fascinating find in wooded areas, adding to the aesthetic diversity of fungi that enthusiasts cherish.

Pittosporums botulinus (Birch Polypore) Traditionally used in folk medicine, Birch Polypore is known for its antimicrobial and anti-inflammatory properties. It grows exclusively on birch trees, forming a symbiotic relationship. While not widely eaten, it is used in making medicinal teas and extracts.

This expanded list of mushrooms illustrates the vast spectrum of forms and functions fungi can take. From the kitchen to the forest floor, each species contributes uniquely to the ecosystems they inhabit and to the culinary and medicinal practices of those who harvest them. As we explore these varieties, we gain not just knowledge for practical application but also a deeper respect and appreciation for the natural world, encouraging a thoughtful and sustainable interaction with our environment.

C: Additional Online Resources and Supplier Directory

In the realm of mushroom cultivation, the internet serves as an invaluable resource, bustling with communities, educational materials, and suppliers that can enhance your growing practice. This sub-chapter is dedicated to guiding you through a curated selection of online resources and suppliers that will not only deepen your knowledge but also connect you with the tools and networks necessary for successful cultivation.

Online Educational Resources

1. **Mycological Society of America (MSA)**
   - **Website:** Mycological Society of America
   - **Description:** This website offers extensive resources for both amateur and professional mycologists, including access to scholarly articles, event information, and community forums where you can connect with other fungi enthusiasts.

2. **Fungi Perfect**
   - **Website:** Fungi Perfect
   - **Description:** Founded by mycology pioneer Paul Stamets, Fungi Perfect is a comprehensive resource for mushroom cultivation supplies, kits, and educational materials. The site also offers a wealth of free information, including guides and research on mushroom cultivation.

3. **The Mushroom Council**
   - **Website:** The Mushroom Council
   - **Description:** This site promotes mushroom cultivation and consumption through a variety of recipes, nutritional information,

and cultivation tips, focusing on the health benefits and culinary versatility of mushrooms.

4. **Shroyer**
   - **Website:** Shroyer
   - **Description:** This is one of the largest forums dedicated to mushroom cultivation, where growers from around the world share their experiences, troubleshoot problems, and discuss techniques. It's a great place for both beginners and experts to learn and interact.

5. **Mushroom Observer**
   - **Website:** Mushroom Observer
   - **Description:** This citizen science project allows users to document, discuss, and identify mushrooms they find. It's an excellent tool for learning about different species and understanding their habitats and growth conditions.

Supplier Directory

1. **North Spore**
   - **Website:** North Spore
   - **Description:** Your source for mushroom spawn and growing kits, North Spore offers products suitable for a wide range of cultivators, from hobbyists to commercial growers. They also provide excellent customer service and cultivation support.

2. **Mushroom Mountain**
   - **Website:** Mushroom Mountain
   - **Description:** This supplier offers everything from spawn and cultivation supplies to educational workshops. Their focus on permaculture and sustainable practices makes them a leader in eco-friendly mushroom cultivation.

3. **Field & Forest Products**
   - **Website:** Field & Forest Products
   - **Description:** Specializing in mushroom spawn and cultivation supplies, Field & Forest is known for their high-quality products and knowledgeable staff. They also offer a variety of educational

resources that can help you get started or troubleshoot issues in your growing operations.

4. **Mycoboutique**
   - **Website:** Mycoboutique
   - **Description:** Based in Montreal, this store not only sells mushroom cultivation supplies and kits but also offers workshops and foraging expeditions. Their website includes resources in both English and French.

5. **Mushroom Man of Peotone**
   - **Website:** Mushroom Man of Peotone
   - **Description:** A smaller supplier that offers personalized service, specializing in mushroom cultures and spawn. It's a good choice for those who might be looking for rare or unusual species.

Online Communities

1. **Reddit: r/Mushroom Growers**
   - **Website:** Reddit: Mushroom Growers
   - **Description:** An active subreddit where people share their mushroom cultivation successes, failures, and everything in between. It's a community-driven space that welcomes questions and fosters discussion.

2. **Mushroom Revival Podcast**
   - **Website:** Mushroom Revival Podcast
   - **Description:** This podcast covers a wide range of topics related to mushrooms, from cultivation techniques to the latest research on their medicinal properties. It's a great way to stay updated on the mushroom world while on the go.

By leveraging these resources, you can not only expand your cultivation practice but also engage with a global community of mushroom enthusiasts. Whether you're looking for in-depth tutorials, specific cultivation supplies, or connections with fellow growers, these online resources provide valuable support and insight into the world of mycology. Remember, the journey of mushroom cultivation is not just about growing fungi but also about growing your knowledge and connections within this fascinating community.

D: FREQUENTLY ASKED QUESTIONS (FAQs)

Mushroom cultivation, with its intricacies and nuances, often sparks a myriad of

questions among both novices and seasoned cultivators. This FAQ section is designed to address some of the most common inquiries, providing clear, insightful answers that help deepen your understanding and enhance your practice.

What is the best mushroom to grow for beginners? For those new to mushroom cultivation, the oyster mushroom (Pleurotus ostreatus) is often recommended. It is robust, grows rapidly, and can thrive on a variety of substrates such as straw, coffee grounds, and sawdust, making it ideal for first-time growers.

How do I know when my mushrooms are ready to harvest? Mushrooms are generally ready to harvest just before or as soon as their caps begin to open, right before the spores start to drop. The timing can vary among species; for example, shiitake mushrooms should be picked when the caps are still slightly convex, while oyster mushrooms are best harvested when the edges of the caps start to turn upwards.

Can I reuse the substrate after harvesting? Substrates can sometimes be reused for additional flushes of mushrooms, depending on the species and the condition of the substrate. Oyster mushrooms often produce several flushes from the same substrate. However, each subsequent flush tends to diminish in size, and the substrate should be replaced once productivity significantly declines or if any signs of contamination appear.

What are common signs of contamination in mushroom cultivation? Common signs include unusual colors like green, black, or bright yellow on your substrate, which are typically indications of mold or bacterial growth. A healthy mycelium should generally look white and thread-like. Any foul odors, which might resemble rotting, sour, or sharp smells, are also indicative of contamination.

How much light do mushrooms need to grow? Unlike plants, mushrooms do not require light for photosynthesis, but some light is beneficial for proper growth. Indirect sunlight or even fluorescent room lighting is sufficient for most species. The light helps mushrooms develop a proper form; without it, they might grow elongated and thin.

What is the difference between mycelium and spores? Mycelium is the vegetative part of a fungus, consisting of a network of hyphae. It is essentially the main body of the fungus, living within the growth substrate. Spores, on the other hand, are the reproductive cells of fungi, similar to seeds in plants. They are produced by the fruiting bodies and can travel through the air to colonize new substrates.

Is mushroom cultivation sustainable? Yes, mushroom cultivation can be highly sustainable. It often uses agricultural byproducts and waste materials as substrates, helping reduce waste. Additionally, mushrooms can be grown in a variety of climates and settings, requiring less water and space than traditional crops.

Can mushrooms be grown year-round? Mushrooms can indeed be grown year-round, provided the environmental conditions such as temperature and humidity are carefully controlled. Indoor cultivation allows for greater control over these conditions, making it possible to produce mushrooms even in climates that would not naturally support their growth during certain seasons.

What should I do if my mushrooms are not fruiting? If your mushrooms are not fruiting, ensure that all the required conditions for the specific mushroom species are being met, including humidity, temperature, and light. Sometimes, inducing a shock, like a sudden drop in temperature or a thorough soaking of the substrate, can stimulate fruiting.

How do I store harvested mushrooms? Fresh mushrooms should be stored in the refrigerator, where they can last for about a week. They should be kept in a paper bag, which helps absorb excess moisture and keeps them from becoming slimy. For long-term storage, mushrooms can be dried, frozen, or pickled, depending on your preference.

Can I grow mushrooms from store-bought specimens? While technically possible, growing mushrooms from store-bought specimens is not generally recommended because these mushrooms often do not have viable spores left, and the risk of contamination is high. It is usually better to start with purpose-prepared spawn or spores from a reliable supplier.

What is the best temperature for growing mushrooms? The ideal temperature for growing mushrooms varies by species. For example, button mushrooms thrive at temperatures between 60-70°F (15-21°C), while oyster mushrooms prefer slightly cooler temperatures between 55-65°F (13-18°C). Always refer to specific guides for the species you are cultivating.

Are there any health risks associated with mushroom cultivation? Mushroom cultivation is generally safe, but it is important to be aware of potential allergic reactions or respiratory issues from spores, particularly in enclosed spaces. Proper ventilation and wearing a mask when handling spores or heavily colonized substrates can mitigate these risks.

Through these FAQs, the hope is to clarify common confusions and offer solutions to typical challenges faced in the realm of mushroom cultivation. Whether you're troubleshooting a current project or planning your next steps, understanding these basics ensures a smoother, more enjoyable journey in the world of mushrooms.

CONCLUSION

As we draw the curtains on this deep dive into the world of mushrooms, it's important to reflect on the journey we've taken together. From understanding the basic biology of fungi to mastering the techniques of cultivation and finally exploring the potential future innovations and their sustainability implications, we've covered a broad spectrum of knowledge designed to empower you, the reader, to take confident steps in the field of mycology.

This book began as a guide, but hopefully, it has become much more than that in your hands—transforming into a companion on a shared journey of discovery. Mushroom cultivation is as much about connecting with nature and participating in a larger ecological conversation as it is about producing edible or medicinal results.

Along the way, we've tackled the complexities of mycological science and the practical challenges of cultivation. We've also celebrated the simpler joys of watching your first mushrooms emerge from the substrate—a magical moment of creation that epitomizes the blend of art and science that is mushroom growing.

As you move forward, remember that every cultivation cycle is an opportunity to learn and improve. The challenges you face and overcome will not only make you a better cultivator but also deepen your appreciation for the intricate web of life that mushrooms represent. Whether your next steps involve scaling up to commercial production, engaging with online communities, or simply enjoying the fruits of your homegrown harvest, the foundation you've built here will support your endeavors.

In conclusion, may your journey from novice to expert be filled with curiosity, patience, and respect for the natural world. Mushrooms are remarkable organisms that offer us a unique mirror into our ecosystems—they teach us about connectivity, resilience, and the beauty of growth. Carry these lessons forward, and let them inform not just your cultivation practices, but your perspective on the world around you.

YOUR JOURNEY FROM NOVICE TO EXPERT

Embarking on the path from novice to expert in mushroom cultivation is a journey that unfolds much like the growth of the mushrooms themselves—a gradual and enriching process filled with moments of learning, discovery, and wonder. This transformative passage is not simply about acquiring the skills to grow mushrooms but also about developing a deeper understanding and connection with the natural world.

The Early Stages: Curiosity and Learning

Your journey likely begins with curiosity—a fascination with the mysterious and enchanting world of fungi. This initial intrigue is the first step towards a lifelong passion and, possibly, profession. In these early stages, you absorb information eagerly, learning the basics of mycology, understanding the different types of mushrooms, and getting to grips with the conditions they require to thrive.

As a novice, your first attempts at cultivation might be met with mixed results. Remember, each failure is as valuable as any success. The key is to maintain your curiosity and let these experiences deepen your understanding. Experiment with different substrates and species. Learn from the community—join forums, attend workshops, and do not hesitate to ask for advice from more experienced cultivators.

Developing Competence: Practical Skills and Problem Solving

As you gain more experience, you'll begin to develop a routine and learn which techniques work best for your environment and choice of mushrooms. This phase is about honing your practical skills and becoming adept at solving the problems that inevitably arise, such as dealing with pests, managing contamination, or adjusting humidity levels.

This is also the time to start keeping detailed records of your cultivation processes. Which substrates yield the best results? How do changes in temperature or humidity affect growth? Keeping a cultivation journal can help you track your progress, learn from past mistakes, and refine your techniques.

Advancing Further: Specialization and Experimentation

Once you have mastered the basics and overcome initial challenges, you may find yourself gravitating towards a particular area of interest within mycology. Perhaps the medicinal properties of mushrooms pique your interest, or you are drawn to the ecological impact of fungi. This phase of your journey is about deepening your knowledge in these specific areas and experimenting with advanced cultivation techniques like liquid cultures or genetic splicing.

Specialization might also lead you to explore rarer and more challenging mushroom species. Each new species offers its own set of rewards and requires a nuanced understanding to cultivate successfully. This specialization not only enhances your skills but also contributes to the broader community by adding to the collective knowledge and diversity of cultivated fungi.

Mastery: Contribution and Community Engagement

Reaching a level of mastery in mushroom cultivation means more than just expert knowledge and skill. It also involves contributing to the community and helping others along their paths. Whether through teaching, writing, or leading community projects, sharing your knowledge is a crucial part of being an expert.

At this stage, consider engaging more deeply with sustainability initiatives. Could your cultivation practices be more eco-friendly? How might you use mushrooms to address environmental issues in your community? Experts in mycology play a vital role in promoting biodiversity, ecological health, and sustainable practices.

Lifelong Learning: Keeping Up with Changes and Innovations

The field of mycology is continuously evolving, with new research and technologies constantly emerging. An expert is always a student, eager to learn about the latest developments and ready to adapt practices in response to new findings. Stay updated by subscribing to scientific journals, attending conferences, and maintaining strong connections with the academic and cultivation communities.

Reflecting on the Journey

As you reflect on your journey from novice to expert, it's important to recognize the broader impacts of your work. Mushroom cultivation is more than a hobby or a career—it's a way of interacting with the world that emphasizes care, patience, and respect for nature.

Your growth as a cultivator mirrors the growth of the mushrooms you nurture: starting from a small spore, expanding through exploratory mycelial threads, and finally fruiting into something beautiful and worthwhile. Each step of this journey offers its own joys and challenges, and each mushroom you grow can be seen as a symbol of your development from curious beginner to skilled expert.

Remember, the path does not end with mastery. The world of mushrooms is vast and infinitely complex, and there is always more to learn, explore, and discover. Whether you continue to cultivate at home, expand into a commercial enterprise, or use your knowledge to contribute to conservation efforts, your journey is unique and valuable. Embrace each step, continue to seek knowledge and connection, and let your passion for mushrooms guide you to new horizons.

Made in the USA
Middletown, DE
10 September 2024

60676900R00089